Raising Kids in the Media Age

BY JAY DUNLAP

CIRCLE
PRESS

To Margie, my partner in raising our kids in this media age

Cover illustration and photography by Anastasia Vasilakis
Cover & book design by Joseph Hilliman

Circle Press
PO Box 5425
Hamden, CT 06518-0425
www.circlepress.org

Printed in the United States of America
ISBN: 1-933271-14-0

RAISING KIDS IN THE MEDIA AGE

CONTENTS

Introduction 5

Chapter 1: What's "Normal" Is Weird 9

Chapter 2: Television, the "Hypnotube" 23

Chapter 3: Media Myths 41

Chapter 4: Pornography, the Worst of the Worst 55

Chapter 5: The Phenomenon of Convergence 69

Chapter 6: Practical Suggestions for Parents 75

Appendix I: How to Produce and Edit a Home Video 91

Appendix II: Helpful Resources 95

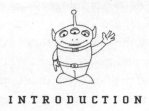

TEMPTED AS I AM (as most writers would be) to make the contents of this work seem like they are all my original insights, the fact is I am standing on the shoulders of a giant. In 1964, Marshall McLuhan released his seminal work, *Understanding Media: The Extensions of Man*. The book you are now reading is intended as an extension of McLuhan's, if you will: a practical application of his profound insights.

McLuhan is best known for the catch phrase, "The medium is the message." While that is a pivotal insight, one that takes a lot of unpacking (and I attempt to do some of it here), I focus on a different passage in *Understanding Media*, a metaphor that is both prophetic and powerfully descriptive. McLuhan said the "electric media" – he was writing in 1964, pre*electronic* media – create a "central nervous system existing outside the human body." Reflect on that for a moment. Plugging into radio or television or the Internet engages us in a *central nervous system outside our own bodies*. That feels a little eerie, doesn't it? Rather "Big Brotherly," to use George Orwell's image. Or, for a reference that may strike closer to home for today's parents of young children, compare today's web of electronic media to the "Unimind" that unites all the three-eyed "little green men" in *Buzz Lightyear of Star Command*, a straight-to-video Disney release from early 2000.

The "Unimind" helped the three-eyed aliens speak in unison and behave in a universally agreeable manner. Is that what happens when our kids are plugged in to the "boob tube" or the Internet? In some ways yes, in others no. As long as they're "plugged in," they're passive and quiet. But once the television is off and the kids need to get along with real human beings, they act about the same as if they had just been rudely roused from a good sleep: cranky and rather selfish. While the media may give us a common language, I find parents agree that even a steady diet of Barney and Mister Rodgers does not result in the behavior we want from our sons and daughters.

Now, please, I do not mean to be excessively critical of the media in our culture. I am not a "Luddite media rejectionist." I believe in living a balanced life based on reflection upon what is to our benefit. No one has ever put it better than Socrates: "The unreflected life is not worth living." And so, upon some reflection, I am a media skeptic. In my professional career I have been a television newsman and continue to communicate via newspapers, magazines, videos, internet sites and other media. I *live* by media. But it is apparent that, by and large, we as a culture accept the centrality of the media in our lives far too uncritically. As I will argue in the next chapter, if you consider what human interactions are like "naturally" and what they are like today in the media age, I believe there's no escaping the conclusion that what is now "normal" is by historical standards *just plain weird*.

This book does not focus primarily on the *negative content* of mass media, though it is impossible to consider the topic without addressing some of it. Other writings deal with bad content, and they have reached a wide audience. My idea is to focus on how the *media themselves by their very nature* impact us individually and how they change the ways we interact with one another. The most important center of interactions in our lives is the family, so naturally I focus on how media impacts the home, especially our children. But we as adults certainly need to reflect on how the media affect our interior lives, our internal peace of mind, as well as our interactions with others, socially and professionally.

As a journalist, I aspire to objectivity, fairness and balance in reporting facts. At the same time, as a reader, I find I am best able to ascertain the facts when a journalistic source is upfront about his or her biases. I am more comfortable with news analysis from an openly conservative or liberal pundit than an analysis from an allegedly "objective" reporter who denies biases. We all have biases, and though we might try to hide them, they always come through. They filter information and set our priorities. I find it easier to discern the facts when an author is up front about his or her predispositions. So here is my fundamental bias: I am a Catholic. I write from the worldview of someone who strives to know, love and serve God in the person of Jesus Christ. He is the "Word made flesh," and his Church is the body that continues to put flesh on the Scripture and give the fullness of meaning to the words he has left as his legacy and our guideposts. I believe in objective moral truths, and while I may fail to live up to them they are what I teach my children. They are a rich part of our cultural heritage and a necessary pillar of our culture.

I share the concern of major spiritual leaders of many faith traditions that our media culture are having a huge – and too often negative – impact on our spiritual life, individually and collectively. The omnipresence of media piping us full of nonstop music, television, web sites, podcasts, etc., can drown out the *silence* that is a necessary part of spiritual reflection and growth. The analysis in this book is necessarily influenced by this perspective – a perspective which opinion surveys and recent electoral results indicate a majority of Americans share, at least to some extent.

Marshal McLuhan is the genius who first gave us the perspective and the language to do this analysis. At the time of this writing, *Understanding Media* is out of print, perhaps because it is a difficult read. His language is philosophical; he creates new terms and uses words in new ways that can be difficult to follow. I hope my work will take some of his piercing insights and make them accessible to a wider audience. I believe his wisdom is sorely needed in our media age.

A FEW YEARS AGO, before we had children of our own, my wife and I were driving to visit her parents in northern Indiana, much of which is Amish country. Often I would take a shortcut on country roads past Amish farms; we could count on passing at least one horse-drawn carriage. We're not ready to trade in our minivan for a pair of Clydesdales, but the rough-hewn simplicity of the Amish has a rustic charm. And it is not only on the back roads where you would meet them. You might be just as likely to see the carriages at a shopping center on Saturdays, especially the local WalMart.

On one particular Sunday, my wife and I stopped for a quick treat at the Dairy Queen in Nappanee, Indiana. We ordered our cones and took a seat. Two families were right near us. The first was an Amish family with a passel of brown-haired, dark-eyed stair steps, six kids as I recall. The boys looked neat and trim in their brightly colored shirts (always a single, solid hue) and their simple, dark-colored slacks with buttoned-on suspenders. The girls wore bonnets and their Sunday-best dresses, modest frocks just frilly enough at the shoulders to emphasize their femininity. The other family was a typical American mom and dad with a son about seven years old and a daughter who might have been four. Their thin, athletic frames draped in Dockers and Polos, casual but fashionable, signaled comfortable suburbia.

But more than their appearances, what most marked the difference between the two families was the behavior of the children. The two suburbanite children were screaming and wailing as if soft-serve ice cream were a form of torture. Across the aisle, the Amish children looked in quiet amazement at their more modern peers. The Amish children were calmly enjoying their treats without a word, staring wide-eyed at the tantrum-throwing duo as if they were observing creatures from another planet. Which, for all intents and purposes, they might as well be, given the cultural chasm between the technologically skeptical Amish and us, the "post-moderns" who often run to embrace every new electronic gizmo.

On the one hand, our society looks upon the Amish as weird, old-fashioned, even extreme. But in terms of behavior on that particular Sunday, who was "weird" and who was "normal?" What was a "normal" reaction to an ice-cream cone? I think we can agree that throwing a tantrum while receiving a treat is a weird, illogical reaction. And yet how many of us as parents can identify with the situation – because we have seen our own kids behave just as badly? What is it in our culture that gives our offspring such a short fuse? Might it have something to do with the omnipresent, high-speed, instant gratification of our media culture?

From the wide perspective of history, it is not so long ago that we all would have been very much like the Amish. Transportation would depend on animals we would name and groom and feed, not on fossil fuels from Saudi Arabia burning inside hulking masses of steel, glass, plastic and rubber. Conversation would always entail looking a loved one or a neighbor in the face, not a disembodied voice traveling over wires or through the wireless spectrum of cellular channels. Indeed, prior to the invention of telegraph communications in 1830 by Joseph Henry and its commercial development over the following decades by Samuel Morse, the only way to communicate with someone over significant distances was to write a letter, which would then take a good, long while to be delivered – so one would naturally take a good, long while to write it. In short, when it comes to the way media filter relationships – or even interrupt relationships – what has become "normal" for us is, by historical standards and by the very nature of how God created us, just plain weird.

For most of human history, families have had no squawking, flashing boxes distracting them from talking with one another. If there was music to be heard, it was either the family voices joining in song or little Elvira plinking away at the piano. Part of the enduring charm of the *Little House on the Prairie* books is Laura Ingalls Wilder's recollections of Pa playing his fiddle. Today, music and television surround us effortlessly. That's strange. It's unnatural. I am not saying that it's horrible; I'm glad my wife has good taste in music and likes to sing along with it. But it is weird, and it does have consequences.

The modern family is so saturated by high-speed communications media that I firmly believe parents need to take a step back and look at what is the *natural* way for humans to interact, and what is a *natural* communicative environment for the development of a child. We as parents need a refresher course in what is natural in human relations. Just as parents can be rightfully concerned about the effects on a child's diet of prepackaged, artificial, heavily sweetened junk food, so too we need to be critical of a child's environment that is excessively dominated by prepackaged, artificial, heavily edited communications media. Eating fresh fruit is akin to children playing together spontaneously outdoors; a steady diet of those gooey, dinosaur-shaped "fruit snacks" is akin to children being glued nonstop to Sponge Bob.

In *Understanding Media: The Extensions of Man*, Marshall McLuhan notes a pattern of what happens every time a new communications medium arises on the scene. The first impact is that it increases the speed of communications. Writing out manuscripts was sped up by the printing press which was sped up by machine automation which was sped up by the telegraph which was sped up by the telephone which was sped up by wireless radio communications which was sped up by live television which was sped up by satellites and cable and the Internet ... and so on. But every time we get faster, we do so only by sacrificing a significant human element – a gift or talent of some kind. To explain, I offer a brief overview of McLuhan's history of communications revolutions; I add to this history an analysis of some of the media revolutions that have happened since McLuhan published his book in 1964.

The first great media revolution, McLuhan writes, happened some 2,500 years ago, when the phonetic Greek alphabet met the paper ("papyrus") invented in ancient Egypt. The result was written language that was easy to learn, store and transport. Writing was no longer a matter of hieroglyphs on walls or stone tablets. Paper would last longer than even scrolls of animal skins. Messages could be written and transported verbatim over long distances and preserved for long periods. It is worth noting that in the fourth century B.C., when Alexander the Great set out from Macedonia in northern Greece to conquer the known world, he took not only his armies but also his philosophers. He exported both Greek rule and Greek culture, which he learned from his tutor, the great philosopher Aristotle. He could bring the culture with him and leave it behind because the Greek learning was transportable, on paper. The Roman Empire that would follow the Greek would use writing on paper as an efficient tool for governing vast territories. The famous roads the Romans built facilitated the delivery of these written messages.

Christians are familiar with Saint Paul's claim that Jesus Christ came "in the fullness of time" (Galatians 4:4). Some historians have argued that the combination of writing on paper and the Roman roads helped prepare the world to receive the Christian message: Christ's words could be more easily recorded and transported than at any previous time in history.

It is clear that writing on paper made communications faster and easier. What, then, about the second part of McLuhan's analysis: that the advance comes only at the cost of some other human capacity? That we gain speed by "amputating" some other talent or strength? Consider preliterate cultures, even the few that exist in remote areas today. They have no history books but they do have a cultural heritage that is passed on as an oral tradition. The keepers of the oral tradition are highly esteemed in the tribe or clan; they have been specially educated from an early age to recite from memory a huge collection of stories and beliefs, usually constructed as epic poems whose structure, rhyme and rhythm aid the memory. Consider how different it is to receive all the key learning about one's culture, history, religion and morality in spoken form from a highly respected elder of the community. Think of the differences between reading and interpreting the written word on a page and the live interaction of hearing the spoken word, complete with intonations, eye contact and body language. Even if the words are identical, the communication is by no means the same. Spoken human interaction includes far more information than the written word. As valuable as writing is, it comes at a price.

When writing appears on the scene, the bearers of oral tradition see it as a threat to the human capacity for memory. In Plato's *Phaedrus*, Socrates attributes to the Egyptian King Thamus a warning about the effects of writing on memory:

> For this invention will produce forgetfulness in the minds of those who learn to use it, because they will not practice their memory. Their trust in writing, produced by external characters which are no part of themselves, will discourage the use of their own memory within them. You have invented an elixir not of memory, but of reminding; and you offer your pupils the appearance of wisdom, not true wisdom, for they will read many things without instruction and will therefore seem to know many things, when they are for the most part ignorant and hard to get along with, since they are not wise, but only appear wise.

In our own day, scientists observing primitive cultures and taking copious notes report being approached by tribe members who ask, "What are you doing? Can you not remember?"

In recent decades, memory has been further devalued as a human skill. Up until the past half century, memorization was a standard part of elementary education. Today educational psychologists dismiss "rote memorization" as "remembering information by repetition without necessarily understanding the meaning of the information. Considered to be a very low level of learning but occasionally necessary" (cf. *Educational Psychology*, Seventh Edition, by Anita Woolfolk). My mother-in-law, in her mid-seventies, can still recite a number of the poems she learned as a schoolgirl. All I know by heart is a few Mark Twain quips, some lines from the Bible, and various Dr. Seuss rhymes that I have read umpteen times as I put my children to bed. Once a staple of education, the ability to learn and recall lines of poetry is a dying art.

Among the few places where memory is still prized for our children is in competitions like the National Spelling Bee or the National Geography Bee. Meghan Clyne, writing for the *National Review*, reports that the spelling bee is a "refreshing" reminder of talents that too few educators value nowadays:

> First, there's the celebration of spelling itself, which progressive educators decry (along with grammar instruction) as an arcane distraction and budget drain. But Bee participants obviously don't: Speller Akshay Buddiga observes that the instruction "helps when you read, because you already know most of the words. It helps you write – you can form thoughts more clearly, and express them better. It helps you in other disciplines, too – looking up words teaches you history, and you learn about other languages and other cultures (*National Review Online*, 6/3/2004).

As beneficial as memorization can be as an aid to learning and a mental discipline, technology continues to drive us away from it. We can store nearly incomprehensible amounts of digital data in computer drives. How many gigabytes are enough? We become ever more dependent on mechanical memory, with consequences for how we think and what we think about. Noting that most Americans can't remember which president dropped the atomic bomb and most Britons can't identify the Magna Carta, journalist Ivan Brescoe writes:

Surveys point to yawning gaps in general knowledge. "Computers not only distract us from contemplation of deeper values; they discourage us from contemplation itself," declares Stephen Bertman, a classics professor at Canada's University of Windsor and author of the recent book, *Cultural Amnesia*. In his opinion, society's love affair with fast and far-reaching machines—online computers, palm-tops and mobile phones, all just for starters—leads inexorably to memory loss rather than gain. (*The UNESCO Courier*, December 2000)

After all, why struggle to remember something when you can search for it on Google?

The shift from memorized oral tradition to writing on paper was but the first of the great media revolutions. The second would come two millennia later, when in 1546 Johann Gutenberg invented the printing press. For centuries, producing a new book meant the painstaking work of transcribing it by hand. In Europe, this became the work primarily of Christian monks whose illuminated manuscripts are now prized as great works of art. Indeed, some monks have reintroduced the ancient discipline purely for its artistic value; on May 26, 2004, Benedictine monks from Collegeville, Minn., presented Pope John Paul II with a newly completed, hand-drawn illuminated Bible manuscript. What for centuries was a monk's standard occupation can now make international news because it is so rare.

A clear effect of Gutenberg's revolution is speed: what had taken a monk years could be done in minutes. The innovation sacrificed artistry for speed; books could suddenly be mass-produced, but not (yet) with the colorful illumination of expert scribes. The most important book, the Bible, was soon available and affordable to anyone who could read; this was still a minority, but a growing one. The power of the word no longer belonged exclusively to so small an educated elite. Society had its first mass medium.

As has been noted for centuries, Gutenberg's invention made the Protestant Reformation possible. It is not a coincidence that the printing press was invented in Germany seventy years before a German monk named Martin Luther posted his 95 theses. Because people had their own Bibles, the charge to read and interpret for oneself without reference to the Catholic Church's official interpretations became both popular and doable. The central ideas of the Reformation hinged on the printing press. *Sola fide* ("faith alone") became a viable approach to Christianity because *sola Scriptura* ("Scripture alone") was possible, since ordinary families had their own Bibles.

The meaning of the printed word is hardly ever as clear as the spoken word. Take a simple sentence: "I love my daughter." Emphasize a different word and you get a subtly different meaning. To stress "I" is to imply that I love her even if others don't. Emphasize "love" and it sounds defensive, as if my love for her were in doubt. Stress "my" and it suggests anyone else's daughter can go jump in a lake. Finally, stress "daughter" and it implies that my son may not receive the same affection. Such a simple sentence shows clearly that the written word is far more ambiguous than the spoken word. Inflections, facial expressions, eye contact and other body language clarify meanings. Black words on a white page remain open to interpretation.

It should not be surprising, then, that wider access to printed words resulted in greater conflict over interpretation of important texts – especially the most important texts, such as the Bible, which is the fundamental source of Western culture. It is, after all, the world's all-time best seller. Similarly, as history shows, the struggle to interpret the Bible and other important texts, such as the U.S. Constitution, results in continued fracturing of peoples into ever more diverse denominations or political factions. The lesson for us as parents is clear: we can never expect a written communication to convey a message as clearly as live, face-to-face conversation. Haven't we all had the experience of writing a letter or an e-mail to a loved one and having it taken the wrong way?

By the nineteenth century, media revolutions started coming wave upon wave. Telegraphs and locomotives made it possible to communicate instantaneously across a continent and reduce coast-to-coast travel from a perilous, arduous, months-long adventure to a few days in a Pullman car.

Photography emerged, freezing moments in time; it revolutionized news media and changed the way artists would see and paint the world (beginning with Impressionism and soon leading to abstract art). The electric light made it possible to do all night what one previously could do only during the day. Phonographs and telephone transported disembodied voices. Music was detached from live performance. By the end of the century, Marconi mastered the radio waves, and in the coming decades voices and music would fly through the air to anyone with the right kind of electric box.

In the twentieth century, film revolutionized photography by recording live-action events and entertainment. When combined with phonograph technology, life could suddenly be recorded, projected and relived. It revolutionized storytelling. Though I do not think one could find a direct cause and effect, I find it fascinating that epic poetry lost its central place in our culture about the time movies became popular; it seems we no longer needed rhyme and meter to retell the drama of our living history. Radio also transformed storytelling and developed a wide range of programming: drama, comedy, variety shows, music, news, sports.

But then came television, which added pictures to radio and superseded it as the culture's dominant mass medium. Radio didn't disappear; in fact the number of stations multiplied. But they gave up the general entertainment programming taken over by television and began "narrowcasting": one radio station for country music, another for pop songs, and others for classical, news talk, sports talk, and so on.

After more than half a century, the consensus remains that television is the most powerful medium in our culture, even though films are more prestigious artistically and books are considered more credible or authoritative. Television's dominance is due in part to its omnipresence: families have the boob tube in practically every room of the house. The wave upon wave of media revolutions has brought us to where our most significant relationships in our homes and places of work are too often defined by the media in our presence, especially television and the telephone, which are everywhere, with music and radio close behind, as they too are portable and omnipresent, and increasingly the internet, where "instant messaging" gives us e-mail at almost the speed of spoken conversation. The effect of the everywhere-all-the-time media stimulation was, ironically enough, summed up by a major electronics company's advertisement a few Christmases back. It showed an entire family with children, parents and grandparents, all in one room, with each individual plugged into his or her own electronic gizmo: one watching the TV, another few listening to music through headphones, someone else playing a video game, another on the computer. The headline above the picture read "Peace on Earth." This is the sad peace of our media culture: everyone plugged in and no one relating to one another.

The telephone, which we use when separated from one another, actually enhances relationships by focusing conversants on one another; it may be the most pro-social medium in our culture. That's because the other media, such as those in the aforementioned ad, especially television, take our focus away from the loved ones beside us in our homes. Television (and other media) replaces authentic relationships with the flash and noise of its programming. As Kay Hymowitz notes in her book, *Liberation's Children*, the relationship-deadening effect of omnipresent televisions has been a major contributing factor to the breakdown of communication between parents and their children, especially teenagers. They live in the same home, see each other, but never have any meaningful conversation. The television is always on so they don't need to talk. Hymowitz points to the sometimes tragic results, noting that affluent, suburban teens with well-educated parents have engaged in outrageous behaviors – such as massive orgies discovered because of widespread outbreaks of venereal disease – in what appear to be desperate and misguided efforts for *authentic human contact* so sadly lacking in TV-dominated homes.

Again, I don't want to drift off into an extreme presentation that concludes we need to take the sledgehammer to all our entertainment centers. The point is not that the media culture is hopelessly corrupt but that we need to equip ourselves with knowledge of how the media affect us: how they change our relationships. Writing on paper made us less likely to develop our gift for memory. The printing press made it easier for us to read books and disagree about what they mean. The telegraph meant we could communicate over vast expanses in a way that was almost as fast as speech, but, like every medium dependent on writing, was utterly devoid of so many of the human qualities that convey meaning and intent.

How important are vocal inflection and body language? You've probably heard of the famous research of sociologist Albert Mehrabian even if you don't recognize his name. In 1970, Mehrabian published the oft-quoted findings that 55 percent of emotional content of communication comes from body language; 38 percent comes from vocal inflection; only seven percent comes from words. Please note that this is regarding *emotional content* of communication. Even if you question how Mehrabian came up with such percentages, the conclusion stands to reason: We instinctively pick up huge amounts of information from all the different communicative clues that are part of human interaction. No wonder everyone from junior high speech teachers to highly paid communications consultants stress all the essentials of effective speech: not just the ideas but the diction, logic, vocal quality, facial expression, eye contact, gestures, and poise.

The media revolutions of the late nineteenth century started adding back some of these human elements. Thomas Edison's phonograph captured vocal quality (though not perfectly), and Bell's telephone and Marconi's radio did the same. Moving pictures first combined body language with written cues, but before long "talkies" would revolutionize film. Suddenly it seemed the whole package was there: words, vocal quality and body language. The sole limitation: the audience could participate only passively. It would take the Internet and video games to allow media consumers to take a more "interactive" role.

But let's not skip past television. The "boob tube" brought the passive consumption of live-action shows out of the neighborhood theaters and into our homes. It transformed the focus of the living room from the hearth to NBC, CBS, and ABC – though radio was first to displace the hearth in many homes during the 1930s and '40s. How television affects our homes and our families is a large and complex issue I will cover in the next chapter. Suffice it for now to note that while it appears to bring the fullest possible form of communication into our home, it reduces us to passive observers. Television is an attention sucker. Its centrality and its omnipresence – do you have a TV in every room? – disengage us from real interaction with real people. It creates consumers; it does not build relationships.

And now we live in the age of the Internet. Yes, the biggest money-making scheme on the Internet continues to be the distribution of pornography, but the primary use of the World Wide Web is to connect people via e-mail; the chief operating officer of the giant portal Yahoo! noted in September, 2005 that 45 percent of all use of the Web is for communication, mostly e-mail and instant messaging. Indeed, anybody who works at a desk job now looks back and wonders, "How did we ever do this without e-mail?" Families, friends, and colleagues create list serves to remain in touch over vast distances. People share jokes, odd photos, prayer requests, news reports, pyramid money-raising schemes – and, of course, computer viruses. Not to mention those crazy money-laundering invitations from "a wealthy widow in Africa." With instant messaging, e-mail can now fly around the world at almost the speed of natural conversation. But note well: instant messaging is deaf and blind. It has the speed of conversation but not the fullness of its content. No wonder, then, that e-mail and instant messaging have as their most dire consequence the luring of unsuspecting children into traps set by criminals posing as young people. It is a most efficient means for presenting yourself as what you are not.

The media giveth and the media taketh away. We know the media culture has advantages and disadvantages, and we can gain power over them if we can name them. We do not need to become like the Amish in their strict rejection of technological advances, but we certainly want to be more like them in terms of providing a healthy social environment for our children, with great benefits for the children's behavior and for our ability as families to live in harmony and express our love for one another. In order to help parents and others reflect more deeply on how the media change our relationships, especially with our children, I will analyze in the coming chapters the impact of television, a collection of media myths, the growing problem of pornography, and a phenomenon known as *media convergence*. I will conclude on a positive note, with recommendations for how to manage media influences in our homes. In the end, I hope parents will feel confident that they understand how media are likely to impact their families and capable of taking steps that will enhance their family life, giving them and their children greater control over the media that beckon them like a siren's song.

WHICH IS THE MOST POWERFUL OF THE MASS MEDIA? I always ask this question when interacting with a class of students or speaking at a conference. I also inquire which of the media is most prestigious and which is most credible. While I do not pretend my samplings are scientific, I have always found that my audience and I intuit the same conclusions:

- ▶ **Film is the most prestigious medium.** TV celebrities and popular musicians all want to become movie stars. TV directors and producers want to graduate to the "big screen." Some say if Michelangelo or Leonardo da Vinci were alive today, they would be filmmakers.
- ▶ **Books are the most credible or authoritative medium.** They have the aura of seriousness (unless they're collections of Calvin & Hobbes comic strips, for instance). They require the most research, the most substantial individual investment of time and effort. I am writing this book to share my research and analysis in a way that can be widely accessible and seriously considered.
- ▶ **Television is the most powerful medium.** It is everywhere. Even if it lacks the credibility of books (or even of newspapers or magazines) and is less prestigious than film, its grip on our society is nearly universally recognized as unchallenged.

Recent research supports the consistent opinions of the people I've asked. An InsightExpress survey from September, 2004 asked 500 respondents about the power of media: TV, magazines, newspapers, radio, and the Internet. A significant plurality rated television as the most powerful across the board: 46 percent said television gave them the "greatest experience," 40 percent said television is the first medium they turn on, and 42 percent said it was easiest to use. Second place went to the Internet, with 27 percent crediting it as the best experience, 34 percent saying it's the first they turn on, and 24 percent rating it easiest to use.

It strikes me as ironic that we are all aware of television's power even as we recognize its shortcomings. As parents, we need to ask an important question: what is it about television that makes it the most powerful medium in our homes? Why does television have such an impact on the people we love most and on our most important personal relationships? Let's take a look at how television developed during the past century to get a better understanding of how it works and therefore how it affects us.

A Potato Field in Idaho

In 1921, Philo T. Farnsworth was a farm kid with a fascination for anything electrical. according to the biography, *The Boy Who Invented Television*, by Paul Schatzkin. From the time Farnsworth first reached school age he felt the inspiration to be an inventor. He read whatever he could get his hands on and clung to magazines with articles on the latest electric gizmos. One topic in particular caught his interest: the attempt to broadcast moving pictures the same way sounds come over the radio. Well-funded scientists for RCA and Bell Labs were fiddling with various techniques to create television. But the stroke of genius would come from a hick with a funny-sounding name in a potato field outside Rigby, Idaho.

In the words of biographer Schatzkin:

One steamy day in the summer of 1921, Philo crisscrossed an open field atop a horse-drawn plowing machine, thinking about television to relieve the boredom, when for a moment, he stopped to survey his day's work. Noticing the neatly cut parallel rows in the dirt before him, he was struck with a flash of inspiration: just as he plowed the field, back and forth in parallel rows, so could he scan an image, one line at a time, with a magnetically-deflected beam of electrons inside a cathode ray tube.

At that moment, television as we know it and all its extensions and further manifestations arrived on earth in the mind of this fourteen-year-old farm boy.

To this day, the vast majority of televisions, computer monitors, and similar screens depend on the flashing "lines of resolution" Philo first envisioned in that potato field. The lines are more obvious on screens of lesser resolution – that is, screens with a less clear picture. But if you look closely at any conventional TV or monitor, you will see that the image is projected as a series of lines stacked upon one another, just like the rows of a freshly plowed field. By the time he was twenty, Philo had gotten married, moved to California, and received enough funding to create the first working television. Though he died in 1971, the seventy-fifth anniversary of his invention was honored September 7, 2002 at the Emmy Awards. His widow, Elma G. "Pem" Farnsworth, was at the ceremony, honored as the "mother of television."

In essence, television is a box of flashing lights approximating the image of moving pictures on film while always coming up short of film's detail. High definition television, which at this writing is emerging as a retail commodity for home consumers, offers images that are as well defined as film. But television as we have known it for more than three quarters of a century has been what Philo T. Farnsworth created.

The "Golden Age"

A chief characteristic of media revolutions is that the new technology takes over the content of the preceding technology: writing took over the content that used to be passed on orally; the printing press took over the content that used to be written by hand; radio programs told stories that previously would have been in print or on stage; television took over what had been broadcast by radio. The 1930s and '40s are hailed as the "Golden Age of Radio" because of the great stars that entertained families over the airwaves: Bob Hope and Bing Crosby, George Burns and Gracie Allen, Ella Fitzgerald, Louis Armstrong, and Duke Ellington, to name a few. When television programming first emerged in the late 1940s, it stole "the gold" from radio, essentially translating spoken radio to the visual medium of television. The only change for shows like Burns and Allen's was that the audience could see a stage designed to look like their home.

Today we find it funny to see just how primitive the visuals were in some early television programming. The camera simply followed people around like one set of eyes. Especially since most programming was "live," there was little or no chance for editing to vary perspectives. Television news hit the air before stations or even networks had established a stable of reporters and camera crews. Programs such as the *Camel News Caravan* featured a commentator telling the news with an utter dearth of graphics. A story about a house fire – and this really happened – could offer as a visual a hand-drawn picture of a house on paper being set on fire with a match. We've come a long way, baby.

Across the board, viewers of early television were satisfied with visuals that today's audience would find too static and boring. One early top-rated show featured the pianist, Liberace. He spent the entire half-hour playing his piano, and that's all there was too see. Liberace had mastered the art of smiling and winking at the camera while he played. Judy Garland even recorded a popular song entitled, "When Liberace Winks at Me." Liberace is credited, though, with one visual innovation: the three-camera shoot. The use of three cameras allows the director to vary the visuals by cutting seamlessly from one angle to another. Even so, all that Liberace's three cameras would show were the smile, the piano, the candelabra, the increasingly flashy tuxedo – and the occasional wink.

Another 1950s ratings winner was the preaching of Archbishop Fulton

Sheen, whose program, *Life Is Worth Living*, amounted to a weekly sermon explaining and defending the Catholic faith. His prime-time presentations on Sunday evenings – always a time of high viewership – were a ratings winner. Of course, there is still much preaching happening on television these days, though it's relegated almost entirely to the religious cable channels. And even these presentations often add graphics and other visuals to appeal to the eye of the contemporary TV viewer. The tastes of television producers and audiences have changed substantially in both content and visuals.

The Next Revolutions

Television grew more diverse and more visually interesting throughout the 1950s and '60s, employing more and more the visual storytelling techniques developed in the film industry. News operations grew and news cameras became ubiquitous, even though in those first decades they had to use large, cumbersome film cameras burdened with big, heavy cans of film. The fact that the film had to be taken back to a smelly darkroom for development before it could be used on the air had a discernible impact on how it would be edited: A typical "sound bite" on TV news in the '60s and early '70s would last forty-five seconds. A news crew wouldn't go through all the labor of lugging its heavy gear and developing the film just to use a ten-second clip; the requirements of physically cutting and splicing the developed film meant you would not have the rapid-fire editing so common today.

Two nearly simultaneous revolutions in the 1970s changed both the way television is put together and how it is distributed. The shift from heavy, messy film gear to lighter, easy-to-edit video technology changed the way television is made and therefore how and what we see. The shift from broadcast-only television to the multiple choices afforded by cable and home-satellite television revolutionized the offerings of TV providers and the viewing habits of TV consumers.

From the Hills to the Big City

First, the cable revolution. The origins of cable TV actually date back to the 1940s, when small towns in higher elevations suffered from lousy reception. The logical response was "community antenna television" or CATV, which amounted to a tall TV antenna placed on the highest local peak with cables running to neighborhood homes. It was the only way for many people from Pennsylvania to Oregon to join the TV revolution.

Over the years, cable and CATV drew the interest of the Federal Communications Commission (FCC), which grants TV stations their broadcast licenses. The FCC found it had to referee between local broadcasters and cable providers. Though cable began in rural communities, entrepreneurs in larger cities soon saw an opportunity. For instance, a company serving customers near San Diego wanted to offer its customers both the local stations and Los Angeles stations. Owners of the San Diego stations didn't want to lose part of their audience, because audience equals ratings, which equals income from commercials. The turf battle went to the FCC, which determined that CATV providers should stick with the local stations according to the boundaries established in FCC licenses, particularly in the one hundred largest television markets. That ruling effectively kept cable TV from becoming a big-city phenomenon, making it profitable only in small towns up in the hills. Even so, CATV grew steadily from 640 providers in 1960 to almost 2,500 in 1970.

The number of cable providers began to explode in the 1970s and peaked at more than 11,000 in the mid-1990s thanks to a diametrically opposite FCC ruling in 1972. It allowed cable to enter the larger TV markets so long as it provided free community access channels for local public affairs programming. To this day you can often see the proceedings of local government on cable access channels. Fans of NBC's *Saturday Night Live* might view it as the ruling that gave us *Wayne's World,* Mike Meyers and Dana Carvey's infamous spoof of people with more chutzpah than talent on local access TV.

Once cable providers met the FCC's minimum requirements for public access channels they could take advantage of the emerging satellite technology to pluck programming from anywhere around the globe. The

FCC gave cable companies the green light to grow; satellites gave them the programming to attract subscribers. The transformation is reflected in the numbers from Nielsen Media Research on the percentage of U.S. households subscribing to cable TV. In 1970, 7.6 percent had cable; that effectively tripled to 22.6 percent in 1980 and has again more than tripled to nearly 70 percent at the time of this writing. The number of cable subscribers has declined the last few years only because satellite TV providers have taken part of the market with their cable-like programming. Now there is a new competitor emerging: we are in the infancy of programming being provided over the Internet, to be downloaded onto digital video recorders (DVRs) such as TiVo. For most TiVo subscribers, today's DVR records programming off of a cable or satellite feed. In the not too distant future, those sources may be bypassed as the difference between cable TV and the Internet blur into a world of "video on demand." But for purposes of this discussion, cable, satellite and internet services are part of one phenomenon: subscription television (as opposed to "free" broadcast television).

We all know what content followed the growth of cable TV: the continuing expansion of the cable television universe into an ever-greater number of highly specialized channels. Sports fans soon had ESPN and its various offshoots and copycats; home shopping networks; HBO and all its spin-offs, with channels now dedicated exclusively to almost every conceivable film genre; networks full of 24-hour children's programming; and of course the alphabet soup of channels for newshounds, with CNN, MSNBC, CNBC, C-SPAN, Fox News, etc. As cable TV spread to the vast majority of American homes it had the same kind of impact on TV programming that TV had on radio. As mentioned above with regard to radio, this is **narrowcasting**: individual channels or stations focusing on groups with a particular interest: country music, self-help talk shows, sports, politics .... (Now, with the growth of video on the Internet, there is the advent of what the *New York Times* says is "slivercasting": Web sites providing news and video of events for an even more highly specialized audience. The *Times* [March 12, 2006] cites as an example sail.tv, a Web channel for sailing enthusiasts.)

The Advertising Dollar

Cable fragmented television viewership. For the industry's first three decades viewers had three choices: NBC, CBS, and ABC. PBS came along in the early '70s and took away about three percent of viewers. That means until cable, the "big three" could count on 97 percent of all viewers and sell advertising accordingly. Owning a TV station was referred to as a "license to print money." But cable's intrusion on the network oligopoly swiftly eroded viewers. Around 1980 the networks' share had dropped to 90 percent of viewers; by 1994 it was 60 percent; at this writing it is down to a little more than half. And that is split among more broadcast networks as well: Fox, the CW (newly minted as a merger of UPN [Universal-Paramount] and "the WB" [Warner Brothers]), and increasingly the Spanish language networks Univision and Telemundo. (In July, 2005, WXTV, the Univision station in New York, achieved a landmark when for the first time it won the "sweeps month" ratings contest for prime time viewers among all the local broadcast stations in our nation's largest television market.)

The year 2003 marked the first time TV consumers spent more to pay for television in the form of cable and satellite subscriptions than advertisers paid for commercials. Research by the investment banking firm of Veronis Suhler Stevenson showed that consumers paid $178.4 billion that year to get their media content, which was almost three billion more than advertisers spent. That is a watershed point: For its first generation, television was "free" to the viewer because of paid advertising. As of this writing, the balance has tipped. "Free TV" is no longer the norm, though it still depends heavily on paid advertising. And with the growth of digital video recorders like TiVo, which allow viewers to record shows for viewing at their convenience *and allows them to skip over commercials*, many experts wonder if we are not nearing the "death" (or at least the dramatic reduction) of advertising-supported broadcast television. While networks and ad agencies struggle to keep commercials in the mix, the future may belong to TV uninterrupted by ads.

As one looks at the changes in television viewing habits over the past few decades, one would logically assume that advertising revenues for the broadcast networks would have shriveled. I recall in the early 1990s when the owner of a station where I worked complained that in the 1970s, network meetings were lavish affairs with splendid buffets offering "shrimp as big as your fist." By the mid-1990s, the owner said, the meetings had become much more Spartan affairs. You can bet we, the lowly paid employees of a small-market newsroom, shed no tears for our owners; we were a bunch of young reporters, videographers and producers living paycheck to paycheck. But the owner made his point: network executives grew comparatively tight-fisted in the face of competition from cable.

And yet what has actually happened to television advertising revenue even in the face of the steep decline in viewership is stunning: Rather than declining, sales have consistently been higher than expected. As viewers know, the networks come out with new prime time programming in the fall. What most don't know is that the vast majority of commercial spots are sold several months beforehand in June, when advertisers gamble on which shows they think will attract the most viewers. As reported by the *New York Times*, the summer sales in 2002, 2003, and 2004 set all-time records. Despite grumbling from advertisers that rates were too high, the 2003 sales were up a remarkable 15 percent to $9.3 billion. And that's not all the revenue the networks made for the year; the networks sold as much as $5 billion more of advertising time as the year progressed.

Come the summer of 2004, the angry advertisers were grumbling even more. Everyone expected that the networks would actually make less money than the previous year. New ways of watching television were further shrinking the number of viewers advertisers reach, especially with TiVo and other digital video recorders (DVRs) letting viewers skip through commercials. All the observers were certain the sales would fall below the previous year's record. Once again, their predictions were wrong. It was not robust growth, but advance sales exceeded expectations, reaching a new record, $9.5 billion. Only in the summer of 2005 did the sales of advertising spots finally level off.

The Hypnotube

How can this be? How could the networks consistently lose audience but increase ad revenues? Some experts note that the concentration of media ownership in the hands of a few companies allows them to keep advertising prices artificially high. There is something to that, but if that were the only issue, wouldn't advertisers seek out other venues to save money? Television must be highly effective for advertisers to pay those rising prices. I believe the reason it's so effective lies in a psychological fact about television viewing that we may know instinctively but rarely think about: television is hypnotic. Literally hypnotic.

Standard hypnosis involves three essential elements: (1) staring into a bright object (2) in a relaxed state while (3) receiving a steady stream of suggestions. If that isn't a perfect description of a couch potato sitting through a series of commercials, I don't know what is.

But don't take my word for it. Professional hypnotists will tell you the same thing. They note that a hypnotic trance is a "naturally occurring state of mind." If, for instance, you are driving along a road and suddenly realize you missed your turn and you don't recall the last five minutes of your trip, that's because you relaxed and the repetitive visuals of the highway put you into an hypnotic trance. Think of what it's like to get the attention of someone who is watching television. You call the kids to come to the dinner table; they remain expressionless, staring at Bart and Homer. You have to work to rouse them from their seats and acknowledge your presence; they're a bit surly, much as one might be when awakened from a sound sleep. That's because you are breaking them out of their hypnotic trance.

As noted on the Web site for the Minnesota-based Banyan Hypnosis Center, advertisers understand how television affects us: "They use television programs to induce a hypnotic trance and then provide you hypnotic suggestions, called commercials!" Children are more easily hypnotized than adults. In fact, hypnotherapists say the best way to hypnotize a child is to have her think of her favorite television show. Dr. Mansur Ansari of Washington, DC, author of several books and scholarly articles on psychology, notes that "literature on hypnosis indicates that children should be either given imagery to visualize a favorite movie or television program, or be told to make up a story in their minds, or asked to visualize scenes with which they are familiar to hypnotize them." Likewise, British hypnotherapist Faith Waude advocates what she calls "Magical Television" as a way to induce a hypnotic trance in children: Magical TV is a visualization that children and adults alike can identify with, you can use a video mind recorder to allow the subject to project into the future or rewind to view past incidents....

> Ask [the] child to close eyes until you tell him to open them. Ask him about his favorite TV programme, then when he has finished telling you, ask him about the part of the TV programme that he enjoys most of all.
>
> Continue with: "In a moment, with your eyes closed, you will begin seeing your favorite TV programme. You will feel calm, relaxed, peaceful and safe. Okay, I'm turning on the TV now, and in your mind you will see your favorite programme on the screen. You will hear the sounds and have the feelings, and really enjoy watching your favorite programme. You can continue watching that TV programme by keeping your eyes closed. You don't need to listen to what I'm saying, you're just continuing to relax and enjoy that special programme by keeping your eyes closed until I tell you to open them and to wake up."

While children may be the easiest targets for television's hypnotic suggestions, they are certainly not the only ones. That is why television can command record advertising revenues even as its audience shrinks and splinters: no other medium can compete with its ability to change our thinking and behavior.

Remember what we said about television being the most powerful medium?

A word about hypnosis: it does not turn us all into zombies with no control over our urges. One summer in my youth I served as a camp counselor. The entertainment one evening was a hypnotist, who sampled the various counselors for "suggestibility" and settled on me as his subject. I was then hypnotized to be "stiff and rigid, rigid as a board," so that I was suspended like a table top between a chair under my head and another under my heels – a feat I surely could not replicate while not hypnotized. But I remember the whole session: hypnotism does not erase one's memory. Nor does it erase one's control. The hypnotist told me I would sleep very soundly that night, but I did not like the feeling of his suggestion controlling me from afar. I fought off his suggestion and had a perfectly rotten sleep. My point is that while TV is hypnotic, we should not exaggerate what that means. Does it make TV a powerful influencer of thought and action? Certainly. Does it render us powerless to reject its suggestions? Certainly not.

The Video Revolution

Recall our discussion earlier this chapter about what it was like to produce television programs before the coming of video. When everything had to be shot on sixteen millimeter film, the equipment was heavy and cumbersome; editing was messy and smelly. The camera was fairly static. A show filmed in a studio with three cameras would provide a few different angles but certainly not the fast pacing and extreme close-ups that are a common feature today. So what changed? Videotape. It gives us the ability to shoot and edit quickly using portable, lightweight equipment.

Like every media revolution, the video revolution was about speed. Though early video cameras and camcorders seem today like heavy dinosaurs, they were smaller and lighter than film cameras. Tape cartridges, though larger and bulkier than today's, were still far smaller and lighter than film canisters. Best of all, video required no film development: good-bye smelly darkroom! Tape could be used and reused to cut down costs.

Editing was revolutionized as well. Instead of having to physically cut and splice long strings of film, video editing involves the transfer of electronic images from one tape to another. Lighter cameras meant crews could cover more news faster; video-editing techniques made it easier to put pieces together and use more shots. The video revolution gave us the style of production so common on television today: high speed visuals that set a stylistic mood or convey a visual narrative in a short period of time.

In the early years of the video revolution, MTV-style music videos captured the popular imagination because they were perhaps the newest, most dramatic examples of the video revolution. Music videos – mini-movies set to a popular song, mostly to promote sales of recordings – became a popular new art form. Performers banging drums, strumming guitars and wailing into microphones would be shrouded in a whirl of electronically manipulated images. The "MTV style" would impact television production across the board, from sitcoms to dramas to news shows. The popular 1980s show *Miami Vice* was famously conceived as "MTV cops." CBS newsman Dan Rather in a much-cited 1993 speech to television news directors complained that "We put video through a Cuisinart trying to come up with high-speed, MTV-style cross-cuts." Rather did not intend his remarks as a compliment. Here's the broader context of what he said:

> In any showdown between quality and substance on the one hand, and sleaze and glitz on the other, go with quality and substance. You know the difference. Every one of us in this room knows the difference because we've been there. We've all succumbed to the "Hollywoodization" of news because we were afraid not to. We trivialize important subjects. We put video through a Cuisinart trying to come up with high-speed, MTV-style cross-cuts. And just to cover our asses, we give the best slots to gossip and prurience.

We can say, "No more." We can fight the fear that leads to "Show-bizzification."

In short, video revolutionized the way television is produced, and therefore how and what is viewed. Like Rather, many makers of TV admit: the change is not always for the better, should not be accepted uncritically, and at times needs to be resisted.

Not Just a Matter of Taste

As DePaul University's Dr. Leonard Jason has noted, one of four children watches four to eleven hours of television per day. *Four to eleven hours!* That much of anything is bound to have a dramatic impact. Much research has been devoted to the impact of children watching graphically violent or sexual programming and how it affects their behavior. Such a critical look at television's *content* is important, and I will cite some of it later in this book, but I think not enough emphasis is put on *how television as a medium*, regardless of the content, impacts us and our children. I think this is especially important after the cable revolution, with television programming more varied and therefore exposing children to much more, and doubly so in the age of video, with the high-speed edits affecting the viewer in profound ways.

Research shows that the flickering light of television impacts the brain regardless of what the content is. A study by Harvard pediatrics professor T. Berry Brazelton measured the brainwaves of newborns who could see a light source similar to a TV screen but devoid of content. It was just a light without discernible images. Dr. Brazelton found that within a few minutes, the infants would focus on the pseudo-TV and their brainwaves would produce sleep patterns, even though the babies were fully awake. Research psychiatrists later confirmed Brazelton's findings in 1982. Their conclusion: "the medium itself, with no content, acts directly on the brain to suppress mental activity." That's why I mean by calling TV an attention-sucking hypnotube.

Consider the phenomenon of attention deficit disorder (ADD) or attention deficit hyperactivity disorder (ADHD). For the past generation, the number of children diagnosed with ADD or ADHD has exploded. Researchers say the number of children diagnosed with ADD stood at about 150,000 in 1970, but more than tripled to half a million in 1985, then doubled to a million in 1990, until in the year 2000 it stood at a whopping 6 million children. That amounted to one in eight American schoolchildren.

Why such a rise in unruly children? What is affecting their behavior? A number of societal factors could come into play: changes in family structures due to a rising divorce rate; a decrease in highly attentive, at-home childcare as more families depend on two wage earners; changes in diet and exercise habits; changes in school culture; changes in expectations of teachers and parents. All of these factors likely play a role. But no other factor is more of a culprit than television. Though some deny or downplay a causal relationship between television and ADD/ADHD, the best evidence suggests it is very real. Let me state this carefully: I am not suggesting TV causes ADHD. Its causes are more profound. But it is abundantly clear that TV heightens the effects of ADHD; for children with a predisposition to it, TV is a real catalyst.

Researchers from the University of Washington published a study in the medical journal *Pediatrics* in April, 2004, in which they concluded that "Early television exposure is associated with attentional problems at age seven." The researchers looked at the amount of television watched by children when one year old and three years old, then looked at whether those same children were diagnosed with ADD or ADHD at age seven. Their findings indicate that toddlers who watch television for long stretches are more likely to develop the short attention spans and hyperactive behavior associated with ADHD.

Another objection to consider: If television has been around since the 1950s, why was it not until the 1980s that ADD and ADHD diagnoses grew so dramatically? If television is the trigger, wouldn't the problem have been evident from the first days of television?

The rise in attention deficit problems corresponds historically with the video and cable revolutions in television. More programming was available for children – though most of it was not more suitable for children – and, more importantly, the video revolution made high-speed edits the norm for television programming, especially in programs aimed at young people and in commercials. It is not as well known as it should be, and some "experts" continue to deny it, but research indicates the fast-paced, flashing images of television in the video age compound its hypnotic effect, leading to attention deficit problems. The cause and effect relationship is entirely logical: hypnotic television with increasingly fast-paced images teaches the brain to shut down its active functioning in favor of absorbing television's hyper-stimulation. After their daily hours of watching television, children (and adults!) are more likely to seek constant stimulation, be less patient and more aggressive in relating to others, and have a shorter attention span for more subtle forms of stimulation, such as reading or conversation.

Anecdotal reports suggest that doctors and other experts who recommend little or no TV for children ADD/ADHD often see marked improvement in the child's behavior. If your son or daughter is having attention-related troubles, don't you owe them the opportunity to see if they can do better without TV in their lives?

So What Do We Do?

Television by its nature draws us in and holds our attention. In a room full of people engaged in conversation, turn on a television and people gradually, almost automatically turn away from the live human beings next to them and gravitate toward the boob tube. It sucks in our attention. For the most vulnerable among us, our children, the consequences are most profound. Countless times as an exasperated parent, I have turned to the TV as an electronic babysitter. Even when I put on a religious or virtues-oriented video meant to teach my kids to behave better, they come out of their time watching television surly and selfish – especially if their TV-trance is interrupted early.

Are there benefits to watching television? Certainly there are, for information, education, entertainment and other purposes. Do we need to be more critical and skeptical of how much we let television impinge on the real human relationships in our homes? You bet we do. Meet a family in which the kids grew up without a television or with it severely restricted and you find young people with excellent social skills. Meet teenagers from a home where the tube is always on and you will struggle to get any conversation going.

Some experts advise parents not to allow any TV on school nights, so our children can do their homework, play, read or do something else constructive. That might be too radical for many of us, myself included. Our kids — at this writing they're eleven, eight, six and three years old — are limited to half an hour a day. So far, that doesn't seem to be too much. TV is also the first privilege lost for misbehavior, and there are times of year (advent and lent in particular) when we "fast" from television entirely for several weeks as part of our religious observance.

We'll go more in depth into strategies for dealing with TV and consumption of other media in the final chapter. But I give the closing word to Christine Vollmer, president of Alliance for the Family in the US and the Latin American Alliance for the Family. In an interview with the Zenit News Agency, Vollmer comments on what she sees as the most negative influences in the lives of our children today; her comments point out the pivotal role we play as parents and our need to make sure the media — especially television — do not distract us from our role:

> I have no doubt that the greatest ill that young people suffer today is the alienation resulting from the growing distance from their parents when they are children.
> The natural cohesion and modeling which makes small children so secure and so happy, and which gives the adolescent a firm sense of identity and of belonging, has been progressively destroyed....
> The absence of the father who works in a factory or an

office contributes to this effect. And now mothers are also much less available in the home, rushing about, trying to "do everything."

The ensuing need for children to identify with peers and television characters instead of with their parents is, I believe, at the bottom of the problems that surface when they become teen-agers.

Divorce, of course, intensifies the effect. So my answer would be: The worst thing is the scant peaceful home-time children have with their parents ... mothers, especially.

"It is not an exaggeration to say that the future of modern society and the stability of its inner life depend in large part of the maintenance of an equilibrium between the strength of the techniques of communication and the capacity of the individual's own reaction."

— POPE PIUS XII

BY NO MEANS IS THE POPE ALONE among religious leaders in citing the need to balance our interior life with the demands of our media culture. Jews, Muslims, Buddhists, Hindus and others can and do agree with Christians that the interior silence requisite for a life of prayer, faith, meditation, and self-reflection cannot happen if that silence is crowded out by omnipresent noise, whether from television, radio, video games, an iPod, or even the Muzak piped into the grocery store or the dentist's office. You might find it interesting to note that Pius XII said the above words on February 17, 1950 – when the television age was just dawning, long before the onset of satellite television, cable television, the Internet, Walkmans, iPods, Game Boys, Xboxes, etc. If his insights were true in the dawning of the media age, how much more true are they now that the media culture totally surrounds us?

Because our souls are sensitive to all the stimuli around us and the ways in which they impact us by changing the reality in which we live and creating a highly artificial environment, I think it can be helpful to reflect on – and debunk – some myths that hold currency in our media culture.

Myth #1 "The Media Simply Give the People What They Want."

If the media are "giving people what they want," you would expect opinion surveys to reflect a high level of satisfaction with what the people are getting. You would expect opinion surveys to show that the values promoted in media content are consistent with the values of media consumers. You would expect attendance at movie theaters to be on the rise and subscriptions to newspapers and magazines to be on the increase – though neither is happening. Opinion surveys tell us just how much dissatisfaction we as media consumers have with the content we're being offered. For instance, the *New York Times* reported May 21, 2003, that 64 percent of Americans find media content inappropriate for children. Among parents, an astounding 81 percent say the media encourage antisocial behavior. As I've attempted to lay out in the preceding chapters, the evidence is overwhelming that the antisocial nature of media results not only from negative content but from the nature of the media themselves, the vast majority of which isolate us from other people, even and especially the people in our immediate presence.

The mass media in our culture are powerful enough and pervasive enough to succeed economically even as their content stands in conflict with the values of most of their potential consumers. In his landmark book, *Hollywood Versus America*, film critic Michael Medved, an orthodox Jew, documented the manifold ways the major film studios have alienated huge sectors of their audience, especially those who espouse traditional Judeo-Christian values. Medved documented in particular Hollywood's antipathy for Christianity. In a nation where the vast majority of us identity ourselves as Christians, that would seem like a recipe for losing one's audience in droves.

And that is exactly what happened. Up until the mid-1960s, the major Hollywood studios agreed to self-censor offensive content: they would not use foul language, nor would they show graphic violence or nudity. The standards were set by what was known as the Hays Code. But in the 1960s, like so much of society, the filmmakers became restive. They wanted to be unshackled from self-censorship to pursue greater "artistic freedom." They succeeded in replacing the Hays Code with the now-popular movie rating system, though in its original form it included only G for "general audiences," PG for "parental guidance suggested," R for "restricted" to patrons seventeen or older or in the company of a parent, or X for pornographic films. Only later did the film industry succeed in adding PG-13, a mid-point between PG and R and NC-17, a midpoint between R and X that would enable more graphic productions to enter neighborhood cinemas, which consistently reject the negative image associated with showing X-rated films.

What was the immediate result of the switch to the rating system implemented by the Motion Picture Association of America? Was this new system of self-regulation warmly embraced? Not exactly. As Medved again documents, in the first years of the ratings system, Hollywood lost *two-thirds* of its regular movie-going audience. Typical weekly attendance at cinemas dropped from an average of 45 million ticket-buyers to only 15-million. Why? As a child, I remember my parents coming home complaining about the foul language in the movies. I can still see the pained expression on my mother's face when she would complain that "The *language* was so *awful!*"

How did Hollywood survive? The first thing that happened was the increase of ticket prices. Ever notice that when the film industry evaluates the success of a release, they do so in terms of dollar revenue? Why not rank them in terms of the number of tickets sold? Wouldn't that be a more accurate reflection of the popularity of films in one era as compared to another? Of course it would. But when you count dollars instead of tickets, today's successful movies seem like the biggest hits of all time when in fact they do not reach as big an audience as the greatest hits of the Hays Code era. When I have to pay eight or nine or even ten dollars for a movie ticket today, it is as though my "vote" is several times more valuable than the "vote" of someone who paid a buck to see a film in the 1960s. Evaluating success by "total box office take" makes films like *Titanic* appear to be "the most successful of all time" when in fact they were substantially less popular than classics like *Gone with the Wind* or *Sound of Music*. In effect, the movie industry covered its tracks in the wake of chasing off much of its audience by swiftly inflating ticket prices, generating sufficient profits to remain a viable industry (and subsidize their gruff, even vulgar and obscene artistic preferences) despite the fact that huge portions of their potential audience rejected the switch.

Over the years, various media watchdog groups have documented that Hollywood's artistic culture operates at the expense of greater profits. The famous Dove Foundation Study looked at all films produced by the major studios from 1988 to 1997. It found that 55 percent of all the productions were rated R and generated an average profit of $11 million. Not a bad profit, and certainly enough to keep the producers cranking out R-rated fare. But the Dove Foundation also documented that the 3 percent of Hollywood films rated G produced an average profit of $93 million! In other words, the film industry was leaving huge amounts of money on the table because of its artistic culture – by not giving the people what they really want. Researchers in the business school at Rutgers University similarly looked at what factor or factors were most likely to predict box office success: Big name stars? Lots of advertising and promotion? Ratings? Ah yes, ratings. The research showed that the only factor that consistently predicted that a film would be a big commercial success was that it have a "G" rating. Which, if you think about it, only make sense: a film aimed at the largest possible audience has a significant advantage over one whose audience is "R for restricted."

In the wake of the evidence, has Hollywood changed its ways? Yes, at least a little bit. The fact is R-rated movies continue to predominate because they make enough profit to sustain the Hollywood culture that esteems vulgarity and obscenity for their "artistic impact." But a follow-up study by the Dove Foundation, published in June 2005 showed a gradual change. As noted by Father Robert Sirico, a Catholic priest and President of the Acton Institute:

> Since 2000, R-rated movie production has dropped by 12 percent per year, while G-rated film production is up by 38 percent over the same period. This reflects the market reaction to

the fact that between 2000 and 2003, the average profit for an R-rated film was a comparatively paltry $17 million when contrasted to the average G movie, which brought in a $92 million profit.

Understandably, an increase in the number of G-rated productions moderated slightly their profitability as consumers seeking G-rated entertainment had more choices. Similarly, profits for R-rated movies increased as the number of R-rated offerings declined. That's the simple economics of supply and demand. But even with these switches, G-rated movies continue to be *more than five times as profitable* as R-rated ones. It makes one wonder why studios would want to make anything but G-rated films. Obviously, they are motivated by something other than profits. Clearly, they are not motivated by "giving the people what they want."

There's also the problem of "ratings creep." In July, 2004, the Harvard School of Public Health released a study showing a gradual increase over the years in what Hollywood allowed in movies receiving the various ratings. In other words, there was more sex, violence in profanity in a movie rated G, PG, or PG-13 in 2004 than there was in a similarly rated movie in 1994. And audiences notice. While many factors are involved, Hollywood has to consider ratings creep and the increased offense taken by its audience among the reasons movie ticket sales in the year 2005 dropped off a whopping eight percent.

Myth #2: "Sex and Violence Sell."

The Dove Foundation data on the profitability of G-rated entertainment is evidence against the notion that "sex and violence sell." Or perhaps it's better to say: "Sex and violence may sell, but good stories without sex and violence sell more." Psychological research offers insights into how graphic sex and violence impact viewers. The logical conclusion from the evidence is that advertisers who sponsor graphic programming are choosing a less efficient means of reaching their potential customers.

Brad Bushman, a research psychologist at Iowa State University, has studied what happens to viewers as they watch graphic sex and violence. His results, announced in June of 2001, indicate that advertisers who pay for the audience attracted by a program's graphic content are setting themselves up for a fall. According to Bushman, "The sex and violence registers much more strongly than the messages the advertisers are hoping to deliver." In other words, the graphic content makes such a strong impact that other images and messages are drowned out in the viewer's mind. "Our findings suggest that advertisers should think twice about sponsoring violent and sexually explicit TV programs," Bushman said.

Myth #3: "News Media Are Fair and Balanced in Their Coverage."

In the first chapter, I mentioned some of the fundamental beliefs that shape my perspective on the world. I explained that I am convinced it's easier for a reader to discern the facts of a story when a writer or reporter is up front about his or her biases because we all have them and every message we convey is somehow impacted by our predispositions and experiences. Among professional journalists, I am afraid I am in a distinct minority in holding this view. It is counter to the ideals taught for decades in leading journalism schools: objectivity, fairness, and balance. But the fact is none of us is capable of being truly "objective" for a very simple reason: we are not God. We cannot be omniscient; nor can we be truly dispassionate. Whenever a report comes from a perspective we as the audience do not share, we are immediately aware of a bias or at least a lack of objectivity. But when we are surrounded by people who share our predispositions, we can delude ourselves into thinking we have no biases. That's why conservative-leaning media outlets – *National Review*, the *Washington Times*, Rush Limbaugh, Fox News Channel – can so readily detect liberal bias in left-leaning media, while liberal media outlets – *Time, Newsweek*, the *New York Times* and almost all other major newspapers, National Public Radio, CNN – are so quick to denounce their rivals as biased to the right. Especially in the case of the Fox News Channel, whose meteoric rise in the ratings has humbled the long-established CNN and even longer-established news departments at ABC, NBC and CBS.

Does media bias exist? Without a doubt. Is it a predominantly liberal bias? Yes, and I cite as evidence not only my personal experience as a journalist and news consumer but also the available research. In May of election year 2004, the Pew Research Center published a survey in which members of the national media and members of the general public self-identified themselves as liberals, moderates or conservatives. Here's what the Pew researchers found:

	NATIONAL MEDIA	GENERAL PUBLIC
LIBERAL	34%	20%
MODERATE	54%	41%
CONSERVATIVE	7%	33%
DON'T KNOW	5%	6%

It's interesting to note that in the 2004 survey, members of the national media were much more likely to identify themselves as moderates than in the past, where far higher numbers said they were liberal. No doubt many have felt chastened by the charges of liberal bias and now proclaim themselves to be moderates. Even so, members of the national media are almost twice as likely to self-identify as liberals as the general public. Perhaps even more telling, members of the general public are five times more likely to label themselves conservative than are members of the national media. That's very telling when one considers what it means to be a "moderate." The national media are calling themselves "moderate" while working in a culture with five times as many liberals as conservatives, while the members of the general public self-identify as moderates in a culture with far more conservatives than liberals. In other words, since these terms are relative, the people you're judging yourself against matter. Consequently, there is nothing in these numbers to counter an observation that is utterly obvious to most of us: the national mainstream media have, in general, a liberal bias.

Former CBS newsman Bernard Goldberg has written two books analyzing the liberal culture in which most of the major national media operate. The titles indicate that Goldberg's analysis is not flattering: *Bias* and *Arrogance*. He argues that the liberal bent explains why many news consumers have decided to look elsewhere:

> There are lots of reasons fewer people are watching network news, and one of them, I'm more convinced than ever, is that our viewers simply don't trust us. And for good reason. The old argument that the networks and other 'media elites' have a liberal bias is so blatantly true that it's hardly worth discussing anymore. No, we don't sit around in dark corners and plan strategies on how we're going to slant the news. We don't have to. It comes naturally to most reporters.

On February 2, 2002, *The Wall Street Journal* summarized some of the subtle bias Goldberg uncovered:

> (Goldberg) explains matters like the strange way anchors have of identifying conservatives as such but not those on the other side of the political spectrum. And so CBS identifies the famously radical feminist and leftist Catharine MacKinnon as a "noted law professor" while Phyllis Schlafly is a "conservative spokeswoman." Rush Limbaugh is the "conservative radio talk show host" but Rosie O'Donnell, who (while hosting a fundraiser for Hillary Clinton) referred to Mayor Rudolph Giuliani as "New York's village idiot," is not described as the liberal TV talk show host. What this says, Mr. Goldberg notes, is that conservatives require identification because – in the world view that prevails at the networks – they are "outside the mainstream."

In short, the evidence is overwhelming, I believe, that the internal culture of most national media – and local media as well – attracts and breeds a liberal outlook that naturally influences the way news is reported. While some would argue that newsrooms should be reformed to be more objective and consider broader perspectives, I would suggest that the best answer is for journalists at all levels to do their best to self-identify their biases so they can be conscious of them in their reporting and the audience can be more discerning about what they receive. Objectivity may not be an attainable ideal, but honesty and transparency should be.

Myth #4: "Because Mass Media Take a Secular Approach to Journalism, Coverage of Religion Is Fair and Balanced."

I understand this may not be an important concern for some readers. If that's the case for you, save yourself some time and skip ahead to the next topic. For me, this is a very important issue. After spending roughly a decade in television news, I have spent the last several years as communications director for a Catholic missionary organization, the Legionaries of Christ. For most people, faith in God is a vital part of our personal identity and our family life. While I would not accuse most journalists of disdaining religious belief, it is apparent that the comparative lack of religiosity among national media and other media elites (notably Hollywood TV and film producers) leads to sincere believers often being treated as "others" who are somehow outside the American mainstream. To the contrary, I would suggest that believers are the mainstream and the writers, reporters, actors and producers who treat us as "fringe elements" create inaccurate perceptions.

Here's one anecdotal example: a friend of mine, Dr. Dominic Vachon, has done research on the relationship between spirituality and psychology. When teaching graduate students at the University of Notre Dame, Dr. Vachon would begin his course with the question, "Who do you think is more likely to be psychologically healthy, people with strong religious beliefs or people with no religious beliefs?" Consistently, his students would predict that people with no religious faith would be psychologically healthier than strong believers. In fact, Dr. Vachon would point out, the research indicates just the opposite: religious believers have far fewer psychological problems than people with no faith. What accounts for the students' misperceptions? Surely part of it is the secular nature of modern psychology, whose intellectual father, Sigmund Freud, treated religious belief as neurotic superstition. Freud's thinking has influenced not just psychology classrooms but our whole culture: the fashion among many educated people is to be skeptical of religious belief or even hostile to it. That is particularly true of the media elites. This misperception spills over into our media culture in a host of different ways, from how religion is portrayed (or should I say denigrated) in film and on television to how religious stories are portrayed in the news media.

Consider the Media Research Center's Special Report in the summer of 2004 and its analysis of major media coverage of religion. The Media Research Center is an openly conservative organization; one of its stated aims is to expose liberal bias in the news media. It does so with careful analysis. Among the findings in its 2004 Special Report: "The tone of network TV religion coverage was hostile to orthodox faiths, and supportive to minority religions and progressive fads." As evidence, the Report cites how the major media, led by the *New York Times,* addressed that year's major religion story: the firestorm surrounding the film, *The Passion of The Christ*:

> [Mel] Gibson's [*The Passion*] was by far the largest anti-Semitism story of the year. News coverage didn't shift from offending Jews to inspiring Christians until February, when a box-office boom became apparent. A much less orthodox product, author Dan Brown's Vatican-bashing novel *The Da Vinci Code*, was promoted with the mildest of factual challenges, without any notion that it was inaccurate or anti-Catholic, while Gibson's film was questioned thoroughly about its accuracy, its fairness, and its potentially violent impact.

As has been well documented, not only did *The Passion* not lead to any of the predicted anti-Semitic violence, but it did lead some wrongdoers to turn themselves into police and admit their crimes. In short, the major media coverage of the film was far more attuned to the anti-Semitism storyline than to the religious storyline of the film as an experience of inspiration leading to personal conversion.

According to the Parents Television Council's 2005 study, "Faith in a Box," of all treatments of religion on television, 62 percent was either negative, neutral, or mixed negative and positive. Fox had the highest percentage of antireligious depictions, with one of every two depictions of religion – almost exactly half (49.7 percent) being negative.

What can major media outlets do to improve? The Media Research Center offers its suggestions:

> The MRC Special Report concludes with four ways the networks could improve their coverage of religion in the future: hire a full-time religion correspondent; hire reporters who are themselves religious; present the religious dimensions of social issues instead of focusing solely on political elements; and present viewers with a balance of religious experts, not just a few favored (generally liberal) theologians.

It should be noted that in the mid-1990s, ABC News did hire a full-time religion reporter, Peggy Wehmeyer, a self-identified believing Baptist. Among her first big projects was an interview with then-President Bill Clinton about his religious beliefs. A few years later, however, her position was eliminated. The lesson: hiring a religion reporter itself is not enough. If the other suggestions made by the MRC are not followed, the religion reporter will wither on the vine because the newsroom culture will view her stories as insignificant compared to "real news." If newsrooms don't make a concerted effort to understand the meaning and significance of religious belief to most of their audience, they will continue to "not get it." (An interesting weblog dedicated to this topic is online at www.getreligion.org.)

Myth #5: "In Music, It's Just the Words that Matter, Not the Melody."

In his early days as a stand-up comedian, Steve Martin would play his banjo and play it well. More importantly, he made it funny by pointing out that the banjo was a "happy-sounding" instrument; even if you sang about death, destruction and disease, if the music came from a banjo, it sounded happy and upbeat. The humor came from the clash of what the sound says to us versus what the words were saying.

Sometimes we are led to think that the melody of a piece of music can't make it "good" or "bad" for us; it's the words that give it a moral quality. But that flies in the face of our experience and some truly fascinating research. The great composer Leonard Bernstein researched whether music was a universal human language because of the meaning – the emotional content – of melody. One bit of evidence he would use is the fact that children all over the world, in every kind of culture, spontaneously use the melody, "nyah nyah na-nyah nyah" to tease other children. A universal language indeed – and one revealed in the melody, not in the words.

Research in the 1980s at Farleigh Dickinson University in New Jersey showed that melodies of different types affect listeners' behavior and development in different ways. Three groups of rats were separated into cages and given different kinds of music to listen to: one set listened non-stop to voodoo drumbeats; another listened to a low buzz of "white noise"; a third listened to Strauss waltzes. These rats were then tested over time to see how their exposure to the one type of music affected their ability to navigate a maze. After a couple weeks, the rats that listened to Strauss Waltzes started showing dramatic improvements; they were able to negotiate the maze at a far faster pace than either other group of rats. The "white noise" rats showed some improvement as they grew more familiar with the maze but nothing like the waltzing rats. Finally and most dramatically, the voodoo drumbeat rats actually got worse at going through the maze. They started off like the other rats, able to get through it in a little less than ten minutes, but after a few weeks, it was taking them half an hour!

Oh, and it's worth noting that because of the drumbeat rats, the study actually had to be restarted after its first couple weeks. It seems that the drumbeat rats needed to be separated into individual cages because they had started to kill one another! Needless to say, neither the white noise rats nor the waltzing rats had any such problems.

One of my friends tells an interesting story about a college professor who attended his wedding reception. While the wedding party, their family and friends were dancing around to popular 1980s tunes, my friend noticed that the scholarly priest, one of his teachers, was making notes on a paper napkin. My friend, intrigued, asked what he was doing. The priest explained that the musical beat corresponded to what the ancient Greek historian Thucydides reported armies used to use to incite soldiers to lose all inhibitions and "go crazy" in battle. Rather telling, isn't it?

The kind of music we listen to makes a difference in who we are and how we act. In Plato's *Republic*, Socrates argues that it is vitally important to censor the music we listen "because more than anything else rhythm and harmony find their way to the inmost soul and take strongest hold upon it, bringing with them and imparting grace, if one is rightly trained, and otherwise the contrary." People in our culture have a knee-jerk reaction against any suggestion of "censorship"; yet, as parents, is it not a key responsibility for us to monitor what goes into the minds and hearts of our impressionable children? Certain types of music, even if the words seem positive or at least neutral, can be detrimental just by the nature of the melody.

A closing thought: many of us in our culture need to get over our hang-up about censorship. It's okay – really, it is. Parents need to be censors. The problem is government censorship of free speech – but that's not what we're talking about here. We're talking about using good judgment in raising our children. As a matter of fact, we practice various forms of censorship all the time. As I write this book, I focus on certain facts to the exclusion of others. Is that a form of censorship? When I was in the TV news business, coverage of any story would involve the shooting of far more footage than we would use. A typical interview would last at least five recorded minutes and more likely twenty to thirty minutes. How much of that would make the news? Usually ten seconds, maybe twenty seconds if the source was quoted more than once. It is not unusual for an interview subject to react by saying, "We spent all that time giving you all that information and you focused only on the single most negative topic we discussed! Where's the balance? This misrepresents who we are and what we do…!"

In a newsroom, the decision to include one ten-second "sound bite" and leave the other twenty minutes unused is called "editorial judgment." And certainly, no news source (except perhaps C-SPAN at times) can afford to let interview subjects run on for as long as they want; there simply is neither enough air time on TV and radio nor the page space in newspapers and magazines. But, in the end, what is the difference between "editorial judgment" and "censorship?" As far as I can tell, it all depends on who's making the decision. Professional journalists claim the privileges of the First Amendment. That's fine; they're entitled to do so. But don't insult my intelligence – or anyone else's – by claiming that someone has the exclusive right to say what belongs in the news or on the air just because of where you draw your paycheck. As parents, we have not only the right but the responsibility to be censorious in managing the cultural content that arrives in our homes and influences our families.

IS PORNOGRAPHY REALLY "THE WORST OF THE WORST" when it comes to media content? Many studies have been done to show the negative impact of violence in the media, and there results are quite compelling. In our media age, nearly anything that can be imagined can be put on display, either through special effects, realistic computer animation, or dramatic staging and trick photography. The result has been not only thrilling displays and beautiful visions but also – and, sadly, more frequently – graphic violence of the most egregious sort. But I would argue that violence is less likely than sex to inspire copycat behavior because sex attracts, while violence repels. When we see a bloody victim, the instinct is to turn away. When we see an appealing sexual image, we are attracted.

In fact, I would argue that sexual imagery involves the viewer in ways that violence cannot. Watching violence on film or television is purely the action of a spectator; one can get emotionally involved but is not actually participating in the violence. With sexual images, on the other hand, I would submit that any experience of viewing tends to draw the viewer into an actual sexual experience. Even if one reacts negatively and turns away in shame or disgust, an actual sexual encounter has happened that affects one's hormones, emotions, intellect and will. If one is attracted to the image, even more so: the viewer has given himself over to the sexual experience the visuals inspire, even though it is a false, artificial, passive sexual experience. A true sexual encounter, of course, requires active participation of people relating to one another in person.

Moreover, I argue that viewing sexual images is not only stronger (because more attractive) than viewing violence, but that they have a more significant impact on us individually and as a culture. Human sexuality, after all, is at the core of marriage, which is the fundamental institution on which society is built. Damage family unity by diminishing the marriage bed and all of us suffer. The evidence is all around us: infidelity and divorce, which has a hugely negative impact on children. Children of divorce are more likely to engage in every kind of risky behavior and suffer a higher incidence of every kind of psychological or emotional trauma as documented by such excellent resources as Maggie Gallagher's Institute for Marriage and Public Policy (www.marriagedebate.com) and Allan Carlson at the Howard Center for Family, Religion and Society (www.profam.org).

The Harms

The Colorado-based Focus on the Family has done an excellent job following the research and documenting the impact of pornography on family life. Consider the following facts in a February, 2006, article they published regarding the impact of early exposure to pornography:

> A number of studies conclude that pornography is demeaning to women and harms adults who consume it. Now we are learning about the harm pornography does to children who are exposed to it at an early age. Even accidental exposure to explicit sexual images can warp a child's view of sexuality and taint relationships well into adulthood.
>
> According to a survey of divorce lawyers, pornography is a factor in almost 2 of 3 divorces. Many of the marriages may have been doomed from the start because of a damaged view of sexuality formed as a child. Daniel Weiss of Focus on the Family Action says children accept the reality that they are presented with.

"This possibly violent, very degrading image or depiction
of sexuality becomes the normal depiction of sexuality in the
child's mind."

And it follows them through life. Experts say early exposure to pornography is associated with increased teen pregnancy, abuse, drug and alcohol use, and a host of relational problems. Researcher Dr. Jeffery Satinover says often the problems arise after years of marriage as external beauty fades.

"The ability to see the human being on the inside and respond erotically requires that you not have set up and trained yourself in a set of completely artificial, impersonal expectations."

Habits

As we enter this discussion, I think it's helpful to reflect on the psychology of habits as they relate to virtue. You won't find this in Freud; it comes from Aristotle's *Nicomachean Ethics*, written for his son, Nicomachus. In this brilliant father's instructions for how his son can be virtuous and therefore happy, he explains the connection between developing good habits and developing virtues. Virtue leads to happiness, he notes, because two truly virtuous people can have a deep, profound, mutually satisfying friendship. So how does one become virtuous?

Aristotle identifies what we might call a moral spectrum ranging from having a vice, to being morally weak, to being morally strong, to being virtuous.

Virtuous ◄ Morally strong ⟩ Morally weak ► Vicious

Here's how to figure where a person stands on the spectrum: Take a situation in which one must make a moral judgment, such as when you see a person drop a fifty dollar bill. You see the money and pick it up. What is your reaction? If without hesitation you run and give it to the person who dropped it, you have the virtues of honesty and integrity. You know the right thing to do and you do it right away; you would not even feel tempted to take the money for yourself. A morally strong person, on the other hand, would do the same thing: he would return the $50 to its owner – but only after struggling with temptation. He is "morally strong" in that he does what is right, but he has yet to develop the full virtue of honesty because he still hesitates; he experiences the temptation to do wrong. On the next step down the spectrum, the morally weak person knows what would be right to do – he knows he should return the $50 – but he gives in to temptation and keeps it. If a morally weak person makes a habit of doing what's wrong, before too long he ceases to understand the right thing to do; he has a vice, which means he spontaneously does what is immoral, and doesn't even think there's anything wrong with it. Notice that where we end up on the spectrum –with a virtue or a vice – ultimately results from the decisions we make and the habits we form.

Using this moral spectrum, consider where we are as a culture with regard to pornography. Yes, there have always been sexually-oriented businesses around us; prostitution, after all, is called "the world's oldest profession." But a generation or two ago, we as a society could aptly be described as having the virtue of rejecting pornography. We spontaneously knew it to be a negative influence on families and society. Pornography was way outside the mainstream. But along came Hugh Hefner's *Playboy* magazine and the fantasy of turning the pretty "girl next door" into a high-gloss lust object in a centerfold. Then the film industry abandoned the Hays Code and started putting nudity and explicit sexual content in films for general consumption. The advent of the VCR took porno movies out of the "adult book stores" and into the neighborhood video rental shop and ultimately into our homes. Today, with the Internet, pornography is never more than a couple of clicks away.

What has happened to our culture? We have lost the collective virtue of chastity with regard to pornography. Judged collectively, I don't think we even qualify as morally weak. Far too many of us look at pornography as legitimate business, something protected by the First Amendment, though the

Supreme Court has never said that obscenity is protected. The high court's problem has been with defining obscenity and pornography – "I don't know how to define it but I know it when I see it" – a problem I think can be overcome by calling pornography what it really is: prostitution recorded for mass distribution. If our laws treated pornography the same way it treats other instances of sex for hire, there's no way we would be in the present situation.

What evidence is there to say pornography has become a society-wide vice? First there's the fact that it's the largest money-maker on the internet. Jerry Ropelato compiled the following "Pornography Industry Revenue Statistics" for the Internet Filter Review:

Size of the Industry: $57.0 Billion Worldwide - $12.0 Billion US
Adult videos $20 billion
Escort services $11 billion
Magazines $7.5 billion
Sex clubs $5 billion
Phone sex $4.5 billion
Cable/Pay per view $2.5 billion
Internet $2.5 billion
CD-Rom $1.5 billion
Novelties $1.0 billion
Other $1.5 billion
Porn revenue is larger than all combined revenues of all professional football, baseball and basketball franchises.
US porn revenue exceeds the combined revenues of ABC, CBS, and NBC (6.2 billion).
Child pornography generates $3 billion annually

In 2001, the Los Angeles Times reported that "According to the industry's estimates, porn employs 9,000 people in the (San Fernando) Valley and generates $30 million a year in state sales taxes. The Valley produces more than 80% of the nation's porn and 90% of its sex toys.

"The Los Angeles County Economic Development Corp. *lumps in porn with the mainstream entertainment industry*, which employs about 227,700 workers in the area and generated more than $30 billion in gross revenues last year. Jack Kyser, the group's director of economic research, said the adult industry's contribution to the sector, while not specifically broken out, is substantial [*italics mine*]."

Pornography is so big, especially in the "entertainment capitol of the world," it's treated as just another part of a "healthy" economy.

A commentary in the *New York Times* by Daniel Jones gives a piercing analysis of internet porn:

> In pursuing love, electronic communication allows us to be more reckless, fake, distracted, and isolated than ever before.
> According to the personal accounts I've read, men and women today are apt to plunge into love affairs via text message, cut them off by PowerPoint, lie about who they are and what they want in forums and blogs and online dating sites, pretend they're young when they're old and old when they're young, ignore the people they're physically with for those who are a keystroke away, shoo their children off their laps to caress their BlackBerrys, and spend untold hours staring at pixilated porn stars when they should be working, socializing, taking care of their children or sleeping.
>
> It begs the question: Has electronic communication officially become the most seductive mistress of all time? (Source: Daniel Jones, "You're Not Sick, You're Just in Love," *The New York Times*, February 12, 2006).

Recall in our earlier discussion the analysis of e-mail and text messaging as deaf and blind. Happening near the speed of spoken conversation, it's the easiest medium for deceiving others – and ourselves.

In Real Life

Then there are the insights of psychologists and counselors. Art Bennett, author of *The Temperament God Gave You*, is director of the Alpha Omega Counseling and Consultation Services in suburban Washington, DC. Art, who is a Catholic and promotes a Christian view of the human person in his counseling, reports that a sizeable portion of his new clients are married couples trying to deal with the wife's discovery that her husband is addicted to pornography. These addictions cause wives to feel unloved and to wonder what else their husbands could be hiding from them, along with all the other pitfalls that come from any compulsive behavior. These addictions have skyrocketed with the growth of the Internet. But perhaps the most telling fact is that these couples often come to Bennett because other psychologists see no problem with pornography. They refuse to acknowledge it as a negative influence or a possible addiction. If that's not evidence of a vice – the inability to recognize evil as evil – I don't know what is.

Pornography is evil? That's pretty strong judgment. Isn't pornography a victimless crime? Who is harmed by consenting adults participating in acts they freely choose to perform? Sure, there have been outbreaks of venereal disease among porn "actors" and even some AIDS scares, but lots of occupations involve physical risks, from coal miners to nurses to professional football players. But let us be clear: pornography has very real victims. Let me introduce you to some.

Diane is a mother who appeared at the National Press Club to offer her moving testimony that pornography is by no means a "victimless crime." Her words as they appear in a Focus on the Family transcript speak for themselves:

> My name is Diane. I've always felt that pornography was bad, that it was harmful. But I felt that it didn't affect me personally. No members of my family ever read pornography. My husband's family didn't read pornography. We live in a small, close knit community. Pornography is not an issue there. I basically felt

immune to its effects.

A year ago in April, my world was shattered by the effects of pornography. My three-year-old daughter was raped and violated in every manner you can imagine by a twelve-year-old boy. When they arrested the young man, we were told that they would surely find sexual abuse in his background. And that this is the reason he did it on my daughter. After a thorough psycho-sexual evaluation, they came to one conclusion. There was a single motivating factor in what he did to my baby. He was exposed to pornography at a very vulnerable time in his life.

What he saw on those pages not only gave him the ideas of what to do and how to do it, but it gave him the permission to treat females in a degrading and debasing manner. Since he was only twelve years old, he needed to look for a female who was younger than him, who wouldn't fight back. And so he raped and molested my daughter.

I've heard it said that pornography is a victimless crime. I'm standing here before you a victim of pornography. My little girl is a victim of pornography. My husband is a victim of pornography. Even my four other children are victims. How do you explain to a fourteen-year-old boy that his favorite little sister has been raped and violated in such a heinous manner?

But I am also standing here before you, and from my heart I can tell you, that this young man was a victim. He came from a good family. This wasn't a boy who was in a gang. He'd never been in trouble with the law. He came from an intact family in a small community where everybody knows everybody. His parents sent him to a youth camp thinking that they were going to enrich his life with these two weeks in a summer youth camp. At that point, he was exposed to pornography.

He is a victim. His family is a victim. His mother loves him as much as I love my little girl. And his mother is as shattered as I am. Something is seriously wrong in this country when we protect the rights of a handful of men to make billions at the expense of women and children.

I dare anyone to argue against the case made in Diane's powerful testimony. Pornography is evil, and it is harmful. As with any addiction, the addict who succumbs to the vice seeks progressively stronger stimulation. For a drug addict, it could be a progression from a cigarette at age ten to marijuana at age twelve to pills at age fourteen to heroin at sixteen and so on down the spiral. For porn addicts, it may go from *Playboy* at age twelve to *Penthouse* at fourteen to hardcore movies at sixteen – and ultimately to physical misuse of live partners, be they adults or children.

In the city where I live (South Bend, Indiana), a group of local businessmen were inspired to take up the fight against the local porn-sex industry. They were tired of seeing strip joints and "adult" bookstores dominate the main thoroughfare south of downtown so they formed a group: Citizens for Community Values. The Supreme Court ruled that what is obscene must be determined according to "local community values," so these men decided to stand up for those values. Committed to doing "the next right thing," as of this writing they can claim ten years of victories, from closing strip clubs to getting sex industry advertising off of city buses to sending a corrupt city councilman to prison to helping a neighboring community draft and pass a model ordinance for regulating the porn-sex industry. They have helped other Midwestern communities build their own local branches of Citizens for Community Values.

Patrick Mangan has served as executive director and chief spokesman for CCV in South Bend for most of its existence. Part of his role has been to go to community groups and schools to talk about the porn-sex industry and its impact on lives. Mangan says any time he gives a talk, he hangs around to answer questions audience members might have. After one talk, a distinguished gentleman approached him and asked if he could get a copy of Patrick's statistics. He explained he needed to use them in court – against his son-in-law. The son-in-law, father of the older gentleman's grandchildren, had spent a long night at one of the city's strip clubs. Drunk and overstimulated, he went home and proceeded to rape both of his daughters. Both were younger than five years old.

Pornography is not a "victimless crime."

Mangan can tell other real-life stories that will make your skin crawl. There's the young wife who was mortified when her new husband revealed after their wedding that he was into pornography and wanted to share their marriage bed with others – preferably several women at a time. The young bride was shattered. There's the man who tried to overcome his porn addiction and did so successfully for a while, then "fell off the wagon," to use the alcoholics' term. This man, married with children, went to the health club for his workout. In his porn-addled mind, he convinced himself that one of the women at the club "wanted him." He approached her in the parking lot and tried to initiate "rough sex" right there in the woman's car. But then he saw the terror on her face and realized he was terribly deluded. He left, went to his car and drove away. The would-be victim had the presence of mind to note the license plate on the man's car. The porn addict went to prison for attempted rape.

The victims of pornography are many, ranging from the distraught wife to the molested child. Not all porn addicts will commit violent crimes, but when the number of porn addicts increases, so will the number of violent incidents. Not all porn addictions will lead to divorce, but the more porn addicts there are, the more divorces we will see. Police detectives know that when they find a child molester, they will also find his stash of child porn. More facts from Focus on the Family:

It has been estimated that approximately 1 in 3 girls and 1 in 7 boys will be sexually molested before the age of 18. The relationship of pornography to child sexual abuse is compelling. Seventy-seven percent of those who molested boys and 87 percent of those who molested girls said they were regular users of hard-core pornography....

The typical serial child molester will abuse more than 360 victims over the course of his lifetime. He is able to abuse 30-60 children before he is even caught for the first time. This abuse has affected millions of American families.

And the reach of pornography is growing. Traditionally pornography has appealed to males and their visually-oriented sexuality, but recent reports indicate the young women of today are increasingly subscribing to the porn culture, with dramatic impact in their overall behavior, as noted in October, 2005, news service reports of recent research:

> Freewheeling young women in the United States and Canada first have intercourse at the age of 15, partake more in oral sex than previous generations and are far less prudish, according to a landmark new report by researchers at California's San Diego State University.
>
> Between 1943 and 1999, the age of first intercourse dropped to 15 from 19 for females, while the percentage of sexually active young women rose to 47 percent from just 13 percent in 1943, according to the study that appears in the most recent issue of the Review of General Psychology.
>
> "Feelings of sexual guilt plummeted, especially among young women. Attitudes toward premarital sex became dramatically more liberal over the same period," the analysis of 530 studies spanning five decades and involving more than a quarter of a million young people said.
>
> Over the same 56-year period, approval of premarital sex increased from 12 percent to 73 percent among young women, while the figure rose from 40 percent to 79 percent among young men.

College-age friends tell me that on some campuses these days, young men and women speak of being "friends with benefits." That's a euphemism for a couple that isn't "committed" to one another in any meaningful way but indulges together in oral sex. Clearly, this radical divorce of sexual expression from commitment and marriage is the result of the "pornification of culture," to use William Buckley's phrase.

A survey of Canadian college students shows how technology is creating a sort of mid-level, virtual sexuality: half internet porn, half live interaction. As the AFP news service reported in February, 2006:

> Some 87 percent of 2,484 students polled at 150 colleges and universities across Canada reported having "virtual sex" over instant messenger, webcams or the telephone....
>
> "We were very surprised that the number was so high," said Noah Gurza of Toronto-based online dating service CampusKiss. com, which commissioned the Kiss and Tell survey.
>
> For some who feel more comfortable approaching people online than at a bar "it's a social lubricant," while others prefer the anonymity "to explore sex in ways they wouldn't in real life," he added.
>
> Fifty-one percent of respondents were female and 49 percent were male. Of these, 53 percent of students had sex over instant messenger while 44 percent made love to a partner via webcam or telephone.

So what should we do? How do we deal with everywhere, all-the-time media that bring pornography into our homes and our bedrooms? What should counselors, priests, ministers or rabbis be telling parents when they find the average teen reports he's "just like everybody else" because he spends half an hour a day with pornography? A problem of this nature requires a holistic approach, and I will try to provide that in the final chapter of this book; pornography as a problem cannot be isolated from our need to be prudent and temperate in our consumption of all forms of media. It's all interrelated. The first point is that, though it's increasingly difficult, parents must help their children develop the virtue of chastity, which helps them understand sex as an integral part of marriage and helps assure the success of future marriages. Beyond that, one practical step is key: do not let your children have cable TV or Internet access in their bedrooms. Televisions and computers should be in the high-traffic parts of the home which everyone can share. Internet access should be filtered; TV viewing should be restricted using the V-chip or digital cable technology allowing you to lock out inappropriate content.

CHAPTER 5 ▶︎| THE PHENOMENON OF CONVERGENCE

AS ALLUDED TO IN PREVIOUS CHAPTERS, *convergence* is the media phenomenon in which what we have traditionally seen as distinct types of media are blurring into one medium. For years, we have thought of radio, television and the internet as different media, but those lines are disappearing. You can see it in the marketing on billboards, on television and in magazines: The telephone company wants you to buy not only their local and long-distance service but also their DSL Internet and a subscription to the satellite television service they own or are allied with. And throw in a cell phone or two to boot. The cable company wants to provide not only your television but also your high-speed internet service and digital telephony. The message is already clear: as far as the providers are concerned, the communications web is all one service.

As also mentioned previously, a new medium tends to engulf and overtake the previous media – television overtook radio which overtook much of the storytelling done in magazines which became available because of mechanized printing which overtook manuscript writing, etc. – and the present medium on the rise, the Internet, is swallowing up *all other media*. As of this writing there are bandwidth problems with the Internet: it can't yet compete with cable television or satellite dishes for providing quality television because it can't get all the information through fast enough. It's like trying to get too much water through too small a hose. But as the technology continues to compress more information into smaller and smaller packages, the one medium that provides everything will be the Internet, or a future version of it. My grandchildren will probably never experience the difference between choosing a television program and surfing the Internet; by the time they're around, it will all be the same thing.

A Whole New World

Convergence changes our habits. I am of a generation that thinks of putting on some music by flipping on the radio or dropping in a CD or audio cassette. But a BURST! Media survey of 13,000 Internet users in 2005 shows that 76.5 percent of respondents ages 14-24 say they use the Internet to get music, and 39.1 percent say it is their primary way to listen to music. Almost half of the age group says they think the Internet will be their primary music provider in the near future. Before too long, record stores may go the way of blacksmiths and ice wagons. The same survey indicates more than 53 percent of young Internet users say they're already using it to watch movies and other video offerings; 65.4 percent play games on the Internet.

I find the Internet allows me to walk away from some television programming without missing any of it. For instance, during the 2006 Winter Olympics from Torino, Italy, much of the competition I wanted to see was aired after my bedtime. I like to be asleep by 10 pm. But I found by going to NBC's Olympic Web site the following morning, I could see the specific competition I wanted and still get my full night's rest. Much was made of the lower television ratings for the Torino games, but if other potential viewers were like me, it's not that they – or we – weren't watching, it's that we were watching on our own time.

No device liberates TV viewers from the strictures of the programming schedule better than digital video recorders, or DVRs, like TiVo. The DVR is a computer hard drive that allows the owner to save programming to be viewed at one's convenience. If my favorite show airs at 9 pm on Tuesdays and I have a conflict, I simply program the DVR to save it and I watch the show at my convenience. Somewhat ironically, most of what I know about DVRs I have learned from the older generation: the first people I know to get DVRs are my parents and my parents-in-law. They can set up their system to record programs by title or by the actors involved; a John Wayne fan can set his DVR to record off the cable signal any John Wayne movie that comes through. Best of all, DVR users can zip through commercials. That is frightening to the advertising industry, so they are scrambling to find ways to include ads that can't be skipped. Even so, the era in which television depended solely on advertising dollars is long past; as noted above, consumers now pay more for media subscriptions than advertisers pay for commercials. Moreover, advertisers are exploiting new venues for their commercials. One major advertising executive predicted that advertising in video games – a more captive audience than DVR-using TV watchers – will grow from a $15 million industry in 2004 to $2.5 billion in 2010. That's a startling increase: more than 165-fold!

A word about what this means for parents. As the media converge, they can present growing challenges for filtering out what you don't want your children exposed to. But the better technology also comes with increased controls. Digital cable allows parents to lock out channels; satellite radio allows the same thing. It's a more advanced version of the V-chip, the technology which allows parents to block the viewing of any TV programs whose rating they determine makes it unsuitable for the younger set. In many ways, you get what you pay for. My wife and I filter out TV programming we don't want the non-technological way: we don't subscribe to cable and we have no satellite dish. Our kids have grown up asking to "watch a movie" instead of "watching TV," because the programming they prefer is what we get on DVD or VHS. But as DVRs enhance the controls parents can put on programming, the temptation may rise to "join the wave" and take advantage of the DVR. Personally, we're not at that crossroads yet.

What Lies Ahead?

So what will a "fully converged" media landscape look like? A typical family will sit down in front of their 9-foot, high-definition television screen and summon a menu that will be more like an Internet portal than a *TV*

Guide. Imagine a Yahoo! page that allows the family to connect through to any kind of programming it wants: comedy, drama, family, news, hobbies, religious shows, sports – anything. It might be live; most of it will be recorded. And it will come from a vast storage facility offering "video on demand," a short phrase that makes video rental chains realize their livelihood may soon be at an end. That's why companies like Blockbuster and Netflix are trying to find ways to partner with cable providers (and TV networks are teaming up with Internet portals) to develop the video-on-demand libraries. One cable company already airs a clever ad showing two small boys reminiscing about "the olden days" when you actually had to drive to a video store to get a movie because video on demand didn't exist yet. The video-on-demand library will be so vast – imagine warehouses full of server-like machines full of video programming – that you can watch whatever program you like, whenever you like, be it the latest Hollywood release or episode number 27 of *Gilligan's Island*. Obviously, like today's cable programming, much of it will be available only for the cost of the monthly subscription, while special programming may be available only when you pay an additional fee.

Some of the first all-media-from-one-box devices to hit the market are actually built into video game consoles. Sony first launched its PSX in Japan in 2004; it is a combination game machine, DVD player/burner and DVR. The sales in Japan were reportedly less than stellar, so Sony delayed its release of the PSX in the US. The device may be a bit ahead of the market, but the market is sure to catch up.

How We Respond

So how does all this technology affect our behavior? One fascinating aspect is that it's not just the technology that's converging. Our media consumption is, too. A "Simultaneous Media Survey" by BIGresearch in 2004 showed that we are developing the habit of trying to split our attention among many media all at once:

When online:
- ► 63.5% regularly or occasionally watch TV
- ► 59.7% regularly or occasionally listen to the radio
- ► 40.3% regularly or occasionally read the mail

When reading the mail:
- ► 73.9 % regularly or occasionally watch TV
- ► 57.5% regularly or occasionally listen to the radio
- ► 35% regularly or occasionally go online

It doesn't take a rocket scientist to figure that this kind of multitasking is likely to have a noticeable impact on how we relate to one another in our homes. If I grow accustomed to giving anything or anyone only partial attention, the communication between us is diminished. That naturally increases the likelihood of misunderstandings, miscommunications, friction and discord.

Media convergence isn't just about radio, TV and the Internet. We've noted that cable companies want your telephone service. Another competitor for your phone service is the "Voice over Internet Protocol" or VoIP, a way of allowing you to make phone calls over the World Wide Web. A company called Juniper Research projected in 2004 that by 2009 one in eight dollars spent for telephone service will be for VoIP. The same forecast says VoIP will become the main source of revenue for providers of broadband Internet service: a projected $47 billion for VoIP on top of $43 billion for broadband access. Go figure.

But convergence will also impact the media we carry with us. Consider the cell phone. For many, it already doubles as a digital camera and/or a player of digital music files. Before long, experts say the cell phone will be a portable television – and that the future of broadcast television will depend on the cell phone and other small, portable units, since the big screen in the family room will be hooked up to video on demand. Think of the cell phone of tomorrow as a video iPod that offers phone service; at this writing, Apple

Computer is preparing to market its iPhone in the next few months. The cell phone could even become a replacement for your wallet. *Wired* magazine reported in August 2004 that credit cards could be replaced by cell phones that "connect to other devices nearby and transfer data." In simpler terms: instead of having the clerk swipe your credit card to pay for your groceries, you might just aim your cell phone at the cash register, zap the relevant info, and – presto! – you've made your purchase. Phones with this capability are already on the market in the high-tech Pacific Rim: South Korea and Japan. So while some of us may want to be old fashioned and stick with plastic credit cards in bulky leather wallets, others may soon carry cell phones that replace your wallet, your TV, your radio, your Walkman, your Watchman, your iPod, your....

What will be the impact for our families? Sadly, it seems that the cell-phone-as-portable-communications-banking-and-entertainment-center can only lead to less interaction among people, especially in public places. Urbanites in our culture are already unaccustomed to making eye contact in public places such as airline terminals, subways, shopping centers, restaurants, etc. But if everybody has their own little TV to watch, people won't even *notice* that they're ignoring the people around them. How sad is that? It's one thing to "maintain your personal space." It's another for that "personal space" to be such a cocoon that it's as if others don't even exist. The telephone is a pro-social medium, connecting people over distances. Sadly, it appears the cell phone is destined to become one of the most antisocial, separating members of the anonymous crowd into so many separate media worlds.

As parents, we need to provide our children the space in which they can interact naturally with others. That will be only more important as technology – which brings all sorts of blessings and conveniences – also brings with it antisocial effects. The more the media penetrate our lives, the more we must be conscious to lock the media out from certain spaces for meaningful amounts of time. We can't be lazy about it just because we ourselves have become overly comfortable with the constant media blather.

IF WE'RE GOING TO MAKE PRACTICAL SUGGESTIONS for parents raising children in the Media Age, we need not only a thorough analysis of the problems but also a clear vision of *what we want for our children and families*. The goal can be summed up in one word: balance.

We want our children to grow up with balanced personalities. We want them to balance all the aspects of our human experience in a way that builds and sustains us as individuals, families, and a society. What are the elements of this balance? Our intellectual life, our social life, our spiritual life, our work, our play, exercise, diet, sleep, hobbies, and entertainment. Note that entertainment is only one item in this long list. Because of our unique talents, interests, and personalities, individuals balance these elements in unique ways. For champion cyclist Lance Armstrong, the balance will include miles and miles of bicycling up steep inclines – labor that would drive me to an early grave. For my oldest son, Patrick, the balance will include long hours of reading, which he loves. For my oldest daughter, Elena, the reading will be less (but still there), while the time playing dress-up and other imaginative games will be substantial.

How do we know if something is out of balance? If one aspect takes so much of our time that another aspect becomes nonexistent, it's out of whack. If I were to become obsessive about a hobby like making model airplanes to the point that I wasn't getting the sleep I need, my life would be out of balance. If I spent so much time lifting weights in the gym that I had no social life, my life would be out of balance. As I hope I've demonstrated in the previous chapters, the imbalance we're facing as a society in this Media Age is that the time we spend being entertained by electronic media means our lives as individuals and as families are too often way out of balance. Because we're watching four to eight hours of TV a day, we have little or no real social interaction with our loved ones. Because we can spend endless hours striving against mindless computer games, we may lose the sleep we need or give short shrift to preparing the meals that make for a healthy diet. Because we can spend so much time aimlessly surfing the Internet, we may make no time for exercise. And because the constant noise of our media culture surrounds us with perpetual distractions, we may have no spiritual life; we may have robbed ourselves of the reflective quiet we need for prayer, introspection and loving God.

Limits

A word of caution: we can't judge what's good for our children by how we see adults interacting with the media around them. I offer my family as an example. When we visit with my wife's parents, we often find they have televisions on in multiple rooms; their computers are no doubt running and probably in the middle of some project. They are the consummate media multitaskers: opening the mail as they sit at the computer browsing the Internet with a cable news program on the television for good measure. And yet when we are at their home, our visits are very social; the media, while at times distracting and annoying, does not overwhelm the fact that they love us and have excellent social skills. We visit and focus on one another.

Does that mean we shouldn't worry about how the media are affecting our children? Of course not. My in-laws are both more than seventy-five years old; in their formative years, there may have been a radio in the living room but nothing like the pervasive media buzz now surrounding our children. Today's senior citizens grew up in an environment that fostered excellent social skills. If we want our children to grow up able to be media multitaskers but still have excellent social skills, we need to create the right environment. Think of the families you know and the children who have good social skills. A brief survey reveals that you know you can converse with children whose parents restrict TV, video games, and computer use. Those who come from homes with nonstop television are far less able to carry on a conversation.

One positive example of parenting in our media culture comes from a most unexpected source. Madonna, the performer who single-handedly turned lacy underwear into fashionable outerwear for a generation of girls – the one whose best-selling book, *Sex*, earned her the title "Pop's Princess of Porn" – has revealed herself to be a strict mother when it comes to media consumption. As London's *Evening Standard* reported on October 13, 2005:

> Madonna is a worldwide pop icon, once notorious for her desire to shock. But as she nears 50, she has become a puritanical parent who is a disciplinarian with her children, nine-year-old Lola and Rocco, four. Madonna, married to film director Guy Ritchie, says she has banned television and punishes her daughter's messiness by confiscating her clothes.

What an ironic twist for a performer and trendsetter who made countless parents around the world want to confiscate *their* daughters' clothes. One must wonder if such a famous parent, having been well inside the media culture, is so conscious of its pitfalls that she is now over-protective of her own children. One might wish that some in the media spotlight might have children *before* they become famous – and so use better discretion in what they peddle to *our* children. (In fact, it would be an interesting study to compare the proportion of television writers and producers who were married with families in the 1960s, when the fare was family-friendly, to the proportion today, when it is not.)

The first step for any family to create balance in the face of media saturation is setting limits. Some might argue that the essence of good parenting in any age is the ability to set and enforce effective limits. I'll never forget in my television reporting days an interview I did with a child psychologist who told me he almost never sees troubled kids from "strict" families with clear and consistent limits; the troubles arise in families that set no limits.

When it comes to limiting media for our kids, we can either (1) limit access or (2) limit time. In many ways, I find limiting access is the easier of the two. For instance, my wife and I have chosen to limit access to TV by not subscribing to cable or satellite TV. We actually made this choice before we had kids. Early in our marriage we worked opposite shifts: she, a social worker, worked during the day, but my job in television was in the evenings. When home alone, Margie could lose a whole day watching the old classic movies; I could lose a whole day watching sports. We realized we needed to liberate ourselves by limiting access; of course, dropping the cable subscription had the added bonus of saving money. To this day, the decision has been a blessing for us and our kids.

We keep the family TV not in our family room but in the basement. The positive consequences are several: first and foremost, there is no television on the main floor: no attention-sucker in the rooms where we spend most of our day (though our family computer is on the main floor where we can see what the kids are doing on it). It's also the case that reception of broadcast channels in the basement is pretty lousy. (One confession: Margie and I have a TV, VCR, and DVD player in our bedroom so we can watch things on our own after the kids are in bed; I would estimate we turn it on two or three nights a week, usually to watch a DVD. We go long stretches never turning it on when we're reading good books.) Our kids have grown up almost exclusively watching videos on VHS and DVD. They don't ask to "watch television"; they ask to "watch a movie." It can be frustrating for my three-year-old, Susannah, when she actually does watch a broadcast program like *Clifford, the Big Red Dog* and says she'd like to watch it again; she doesn't understand that we don't have it on tape or disc. But the small frustration is well worth the control it gives us over media content.

For the Internet, we have chosen to use a filtered Internet provider.

Last time I checked there were more than seventy companies offering this service, either by dial-up or broadband. What comes to our computer is filtered for violence, obscenity and other negatives even before our kids have a chance to access it. Filtering software that cleans the content as it comes into your computer is a positive option as well, though it may not be as thorough and is easier for Web-savvy teens to circumvent. Major Internet providers also allow you to put parental controls in place. Whichever way you do it, be aware there's no perfect filtering system; not much slips through, but they will keep you from finding some things that may not be offensive. Regardless, the positives for the family far outweigh any possible inconvenience. In short, whether on TV or the computer, I believe the most effective way to limit negative content is to make sure it never comes into your house in the first place.

Even with these content restrictions, we still need to place *time limits* on media consumption. On a typical day, my kids can each spend half an hour on the computer (usually playing a game) and watch a half-hour video. When they get in trouble, usually the first privilege they lose is media-related, either movies or the computer, depending on which medium is more attractive to which child. Some parents may think that's too restrictive, but others may think it's too loose. In his book, *The Educated Child*, former U.S. Secretary of Education William Bennett advocates no television at all on school nights. That certainly makes sense for children who have much homework to do. An active teenager involved in sports or other positive extracurriculars probably has little or no time for television. A teen who spends endless hours on the Internet or watching TV, however, is a teen in need of loving structure and attention. Or, as the teens themselves might put it, he or she needs to "get a life."

Focus on the Family offered the following suggestion in answering the question; how can we best manage television in our home? The strategy they suggest applies to video games and other media as well:

It seems that we have three objectives as parents: First, we want to monitor the quality of the programs our children watch. Second, we want to regulate the quantity of television they see. Even good programs may have an undesirable influence on the rest of children's activities if they spend too much time watching them. Third, we should include the entire family in establishing a TV policy.

I read about a system recently that is very effective in accomplishing all three of these purposes. First, it was suggested that parents sit down with the children and agree upon a list of approved programs that are appropriate for each age level. Then type that list (or at least write it clearly) and enclose it in clear plastic so it can be referred to throughout the week.

Second, either purchase or make a roll of tickets. Issue each child 10 tickets per week, and let him or her use them to "buy" the privilege of watching the programs on the approved list. When the tickets are gone, television viewing is over for that week. This teaches a child to be discriminating about what is watched. A maximum of 10 hours of viewing per week might be an appropriate place to start, compared with the national average of 40 to 50 hours per week. That's far too much, especially for an elementary school child.

Strategies

For little ones, restricting media will mean they spend more time playing. Parents have to realize that's going to mean more noise around the house and, at first, probably more fighting as the kids work their way towards better social skills. You will definitely have to do some refereeing. In the long run it will be worth it as you see your children improve in their social interactions and use their free time more creatively. In today's smaller families, parents may have to help a child build up his or her network of friends with a steady diet of play dates. (Of course, you could always have more kids, giving the ones you have playmates for life and yourselves a greater pool of family love. Not to mention more citizens to help pay for baby boomers' social security!) For older children, the time limits are likely to mean more minivan time for you driving the kids to various activities. Most importantly, it has to mean we spend more time in real, interpersonal exchanges with our children. We have to take the time and initiative to get our kids talking to us and to one another.

One important barometer of the communication in a family – with clear connections to how our children behave – is the frequency of family dinners. Consider the following research published in September 2005 by Columbia University's Center on Addiction and Substance Abuse (CASA) as reported by The Howard Center for Family, Religion and Society:

> CASA conducted a telephone survey of 1,000 teens, ages 12 to 17, and 829 parents of teens in the spring of 2005 to iden- tify factors that increase the risk of adolescent use of cigarettes, alcohol, and illegal drugs, including marijuana. Confirming a more statistically rigorous study at the University of Minnesota that documented the protective nature of regular family meals in tempering risky behaviors, CASA discovered that teens who are home for dinner at least five times per week - relative to teens who have no more than two family meals per week - are also more likely to rate their family dinners as high quality.
>
> Of teens that dine infrequently with their parents, *45 per- cent say the television is usually on when they do eat together, 29 percent say the family does not talk very much, and 16 percent lament that their dinners are often cut short*. But among the teens who frequently eat with the family at home, only 34 percent say the television is on, only 12 percent say the family does not talk much, and only 5 percent think that their dinners do not last long enough.
>
> The frequency of family dinners also appears to improve the quality of family relations, not just the dinners. Relative to teens

who have infrequent family meals, their peers from families with a regular dinner time not only report less tension in the home, but are also *more likely to approach their mother or father or both when confronting a serious problem*. They also are more likely to say that their parents are "very proud" of them [*italics mine*].

In summation: it's important for our children that we as parents not only provide the irreplaceable communications environment of family dinners but that we emphasize real interaction by turning off the attention-sucking hypnotube.

As an aside: Am I the only one who hates going out to eat with my wife and being surrounded by televisions at every conceivable viewing angle? Why do restaurants think they need to besiege their patrons with distractions? I don't want to be distracted by the attention-sucker. I want to focus on my lovely bride. Harumph. One of our first criteria for choosing a restaurant on a date night is whether or not it has televisions. I hope some restaurant managers (and chains!) read this and reconsider their policies.

Projects

Along with family dinners, family projects need to help fill the time that too easily gets consumed by the hypnotube. It's like the Gospel story in which Jesus warns that getting rid of one demon can leave a soul ripe for invasion by something even worse. We need to make sure media limits don't result in idle time and corresponding mischief.

The projects we undertake with our kids can be as simple and spur-of-the-moment as reading a book to a little one – or having a book read to you by the elementary student who's just learning how. They can be craft projects for holidays or seasons, or home-based science projects. My six-year-old, Leo, loves bugs; he's fascinated by the ant farm he got for Christmas. Watching the ants interact beats the heck out of watching the Power Rangers.

For children age twelve and up, I recommend a family project that will help them watch television and movies more critically. In our student days, I think we've all had the experience of an explanation that demystifies part of the world around us. I remember in particular how an understanding of plot development, character development and the use of symbols helped me understand why a piece of literature affected me in a particularly poignant way. I recall a sense of loss, because understanding the parts made me less susceptible to the impact of the whole. Reading became more scientific, less romantic. It also meant I was less likely to be manipulated by it. Whether it was a story, a poem, some music, or a piece of visual art, the ability to understand how the artist achieved the end made my appreciation of it less innocent but more mature. We become less naïve and more capable of critical thinking.

We as parents can help our children be more critical consumers of media by working with them to create media. In particular, I'm thinking of a family project to create a short film or video. The goal is to help our children understand how a video is put together so they can watch a program more critically. The more attentive they are to the elements of production, the more intelligently they will watch and the less likely they are to watch as idle couch potatoes.

Start by studying some short films. I think the best examples to use are commercials. A video search for "Super Bowl commercial" or even "funny commercial" on any of the major search engines will produce a number of entertaining ads you can review over and over with your children. Of course, you'll want to do the search on your own first and make sure you have good examples to use and that nothing inappropriate will appear. You can probably even save the short videos to your computer so you have them ready and don't have to search all over again when showing them to your kids. You could also record some sets of commercials on tape or on your DVR, depending on what technology is available to you. I find using ads already available on the Internet is easiest.

When you've chosen the ads you want, go over them with your kids. First, watch them through and enjoy the humor. But then go back again over each one a few times. Note how long the ad is: usually thirty seconds if from the U.S., but those from other countries may be longer. Then count how many edits you see in the ad; see how many times the video cuts to a different shot or a different angle. You will find that most commercials keep the action moving by using fifteen to twenty or even more edits in a quick thirty seconds; that means the average shot lasts on camera less than two seconds, and many shots are just a fraction of a second. With the fast pace of the shots, take notice of whether the camera is ever panning across or zooming in. When amateurs first get their hands on a video camera, they instinctively want to pan and zoom all over the place. What your quick review of commercials will show, however, is that to create a fast-paced visual narrative you want clear, steady shots from a variety of angles, not a bunch of pans and zooms. If the video is clear, our eyes are accustomed to identifying a scene in less than a second. Editors take advantage of this to create a visual story with good, clear shots from various angles and little or no zooming and panning.

Discuss what you see with your child. Do they see how the camera angles work to tell the story? Do they understand that steady shots are more useful for editing than pans and zooms? Do they see that letting the action go through the frame (such as a person walking in then out of view) is effective and makes editing easier than if the camera always follows the action?

Once you've studied how a short piece such as a commercial is put together, you can undertake a family project to see if you can do it. I explain some ways to do so in Appendix I of this book.

So now you and your children have a completed project. What have you learned? You've discovered why directors and their camera operators work hard to get different angles. You've made yourselves aware of what it takes to tell a visual story smoothly and without distracting jump cuts. You've found out what it's like to add words or music to video. You've told a story, and I hope you've had a lot of fun doing it. In the process, you've also opened your children's minds to what goes into composing and editing any film or video production. They have become more informed and more critical consumers of visual media. They will no longer be so mystified by the magic of movies and television; they will have lost that "naïve innocence" but gained a critical maturity in the way they can watch a program. You can make side comments to one another about how certain camera angles are used effectively in a movie you're watching. You can become aware of how lighting might affect what you show and how important good lighting is, especially when you want to show clear detail. Ultimately, your children may watch some programs and realize how poorly done they are. They might even get up and walk away from the junk that beforehand they might mindlessly absorb. And who knows? Video production might become your child's hobby and lead in future years to something more substantial. My college roommate, a film major, never achieved his Hollywood dreams, but he has made fine living for his family in the advertising industry. And, of course, I managed to earn a living wage making television news reports. Video has become the language of our culture; for you and your kids to become "video literate" is a wise move for a whole host of reasons.

Gauging Parent-Child Communication

Working together on a project like producing a short video is bound to get parents and children communicating with one another. I am convinced that is the true measure of whether or not the media presence in our home has thrown our lives out of balance: are we communicating? A book popular in the 1970s, *Why Am I Afraid to Tell You Who I Am?* by John Powell, SJ, tells of five levels of communication that are a great tool for analyzing how well we're communicating with others, especially family members. The levels in descending order are:

1. **Cliché conversation**: This is simply the traditional greeting we give one another. We say, "Hi, how are you?" We do not, however, expect the other person to then list specific medical diagnoses. The question is a cliché that simply acknowledges another person. Answering with lots of detail is considered rude and inappropriate.

2. **Talking about others**: This is idle chitchat about what's happening in the world. Unlike cliché conversation, this level invites conversation but at a superficial level. In my family, this is almost always talking about the weather. I call my parents every Sunday, and even though we want to share at a deep level, it seems by habit we always have to talk about the weather first. This level can often be idle chatter about sports or about people you know, even characters in a movie or television program. At its worst, this level of communication descends into nasty gossip.

3. **Sharing my thoughts**: This is the first level at which one actually opens up and reveals something about oneself. Among friends, this can flow naturally out of level 4: you start off chatting about others but soon begin to offer observations that show what's on your mind. Some people, though, come to this level and want to go no further. I have a friend who often voices his views and then says, "But that's just me!" What he's really saying is: I hold these views and I don't want you to comment on them, so I'm cutting off the conversation at this juncture.

4. **Sharing my feelings**: This is the level at which we share what we really feel, what we really care about. Communicating at this level is possible when people have a relationship and a good measure of trust. Note that the descending levels tend to flow from one to the other. Have you ever met a stranger who started telling you some of the most important things happening in his or her personal life? Remember how odd, even spooky that felt? That's the case of someone going straight to level 4 communication without navigating the previous levels, which help prepare us for more intimate, more revealing communication.

5. **Peak communication**: This is our goal. Peak communication occurs when two or more people "really connect" by sharing their thoughts and feelings in mutual respect and love for one another. Those of us who are married should experience this fairly frequent-

ly – and if not, we need to be spending more one-on-one time with our spouses. But certainly we can all recall the time when we were courting and we found that we were able to communicate with one another in a joyful, loving, open, honest and thrilling way. It's called falling in love. Now, we can't expect to live in a constant state of peak communication, just as we can't expect to live in a constant state of euphoria. But we should be having peak communication experiences with those we love at least every month or so.

Think of your relationships with your children in terms of these five levels. Do you ever have more than cliché communication? Do you know what things your kids like to talk about so you can get them chatting (level 2)? Can you share your thoughts in an open manner so that your child will respond in kind (level 3)? Can you do the same with your feelings (level 4)? Do you and your children ever get to where you seem to really connect in what we would call peak communication?

If you find you do not communicate with your children at a very deep level, how much of it is because you allow the constant drone of the media to distract everyone in your home? What steps do you need to take to create an environment in which you and your loved ones really can communicate with one another? How much work do you need to do to start navigating through the five levels of communication with each member of your family?

Obstacles in Our Hearts

Clearing out the media clutter in our lives is like sorting through the attic where we've stuffed all the junk we never throw away. We have a way of filling our homes with "things" we think we may use some day or which may have a use in some conceivable situation – but that situation somehow never arises, does it? Just like the organizational experts who get paid lots of money to help people sort through their clutter and straighten up their homes, we need to go through our media habits, get organized and take steps to focus on what's most important: our family relationships.

We may have the best of intentions in this regard, but because of our human nature we need to be wary of certain pitfalls. We are prone to pride: instead of looking at ourselves honestly and critically, we can say, "Well, I'm doing okay, especially compared to *that family over there*...." To which we all must say: show some humility and lose the pride. Don't measure yourself or your family against what you think is happening in other homes. Do your best to assess how things really are in your own home and then do what you can to make it better.

The next pitfall: being too comfortable. Why do we spend hours watching television, playing video games or surfing the Internet? Because it's pleasant. It's comfortable. Breaking out of pleasing, comfortable habits is extremely challenging, but we have to look realistically at what's really good for our families. No sane parent raises a child according to the pleasure principle: "If it feels good, do it." That's a recipe for disaster for adults, let alone the immature. Parenting is more like a physical workout: no pain, no gain. Love calls for sacrifice. To really love my children, I need to deny myself certain pleasures in order to do what's best for them. Every parent instinctively knows this. How do I apply it to the consumption of media in our home?

The final big obstacle: Fear that we're going to seem "weird" or out of touch, or that our kids will become "nerds" and "outcasts" because they're not up on the latest TV shows, movies, video games, etc. We have to ask ourselves: do we really want our home governed by the standards of the anonymous crowd? Do we have to "keep up with the Joneses?" Or do we find that we actually get along better with the Joneses when we can just chat and laugh together and have our children play together, rather than playing the game of consumer one-upmanship?

The Ultimate Goal

As I mentioned at the beginning of this chapter, the goal is balance. There are so many different elements to our lives; media and entertainment have a role, but the time they take should definitely be a minority share. In the age of TV and the Internet, media have grown out of proportion to take the lion's share of our time. For the sake of our marriages and our families, we can't let that continue.

Marshal McLuhan predicted in 1964 that in the future, parents and educators would strive to protect themselves and their children from "media fallout," just as people in the 1950s and '60s were building bomb shelters to protect themselves in case of nuclear fallout from atomic warfare. Are we protecting ourselves from media fallout? I think many in our society are. At the beginning of the book we talked about the Amish; they are an extreme example of a people who protect themselves from all sorts of cultural "fall-out." But I would submit that the homeschooling movement that has exploded in our culture over the past generation is probably the best example of reacting against cultural fallout – and that means media fallout. Millions of loving families have taken their children out of schools, be they public or private, secular or religious, in order to take full responsibility for their children's upbringing.

What have been the results? Despite the fears of establishment educators, all indications are that homeschooling is extremely successful. We've all seen homeschoolers take over the top spots at the national spelling bees and geography bees. That said, my wife and I do not homeschool. We have not felt called to do so, but we have great admiration for our many friends who do. Homeschooling has gone from what seemed like fringe element among extremists to a viable, mainstream option for many families. And it clearly is a rejection of our culture's "media fallout."

My children attend our parish Catholic school so they can be in an environment that supports the values we hold most dear. We limit the media in our home both according to access and according to time. We are trying to practice what I preach in this book: balance! It's not easy and it can involve many shades of gray. For instance, when a child has the flu and is in bed for the day, he or she can have a small, portable, nine-inch TV to watch the programs on PBS. Obviously, that's an exceptional situation. The main thing is that we have clear limits and that we stick to them consistently. It's to the point where the kids have become good about policing themselves and each other with regard to keeping the media in perspective. And we love to see the many creative ways they find to play together.

Ultimately, I believe the greatest risk posed by our media culture is the drowning out of the still, small voice in each of our souls that is our true identity before our God and Creator. What relationship is more important than our relationship with the God who loves us enough to give us life, watch us falter, and offer us forgiveness to get up again and keep trying to do better? All love begins with God, who is Love. A truly loving family – one whose lives are in balance – begins as a family that prays together and worships God together. They can talk about God together. That is the real recipe for peak communication. And the constant noise of the media culture is a real threat to the interior peace we need to pray and to love God.

Again, this is not a call to be a media rejectionist. The various media are amazing and wonderful in many ways. Professionally, people like me live by the media. But we need to be critical of the media and their place in our lives. What person can claim to be truly free if he or she cannot moderate the media influence in his or her life?

May God bless you and your family. And may you exercise so much control over the media in your household that you grow ever closer in love through working, playing and praying together with deep, joyful, heartfelt communication.

APPENDIX I: ▶| HOW TO PRODUCE AND EDIT A HOME VIDEO

BEGIN BY TALKING WITH YOUR CHILD OR CHILDREN about the process of *building a sequence*. Look again at one or more of the commercials and see how the several quick shots tell a story by being put in a logical sequence. As you start to get a sense of how the visual sequence tells a story, start to talk with your child or children about a story you could tell together. You could take it from a favorite children's book of theirs or take something cute and funny that your kids do and turn it into a short movie, perhaps thirty to sixty seconds long. The more familiar everyone is with the story you're telling, the easier it will be for everyone to participate. Maybe you'll find a way to tell the story of *Goldilocks and the Three Bears* in thirty to forty seconds, or maybe you'll show what happens when the three year old tries to play ring-around-the-rosy with the family dog. Whatever you choose, it should be something that is easily repeated so you can use your one camera to shoot it from different angles and get all the elements you need for the sequence to come together with the pacing of a big-time commercial.

There are two ways to shoot and edit a home video. The first is called "editing in the camera." In this system, you shoot all the scenes in sequence and have your completed video once you're done shooting. That may sound simple but it eliminates the opportunity to do the hands-on editing that can help your children see how professional videos are put together. It also wipes out your ability to redo a shot. The other, better way is to shoot the video in pieces, even shooting several takes, with the goal of downloading the footage onto your computer and editing the final product with a software program designed for making videos. I'll explain in more detail what this entails and I think you'll see why this is a better educational process for you and your kids.

An important tip if you're going the preferred route of editing on the computer: even if you plan to use three seconds of a shot or less, be sure while recording each video clip to let the camera run for at least ten seconds. You'll find when editing that you often need the full ten seconds in order to make sure you can select the precise frames you really need. Also, for every camera angle you use, think of getting a wide shot of the action, a medium shot and then various tight shots. The different angles and different degrees of tightness will allow you to edit together seamlessly some shots that otherwise might appear to have been shot at different times – which, of course, they have been, but your goal is to put them together as though you had half a dozen cameras simultaneously videotaping a single, live event.

One more videography tip: make sure the light source is behind you. Don't shoot into the light. The camcorder records contrast, and a bright light in the lens will make everything else turn out dark. Keep the light source behind your camera and focused on the subject you're shooting. If possible, the best lighting for a video project is outside on an overcast day. That gives you the best soft, diffuse lighting for your video, and it's evenly distributed from every angle. Obviously, there is much more to learn as far as expert lighting, but these few tips are the essentials you'll need as a beginner.

Once you've decided on the visual story you want to tell and you've gotten good video of it from a variety of angles, you'll need to download the images from your camcorder onto your computer. Your camcorder, if it is at all recent, likely came with a cord that allows you to connect to your computer's USB port. If you don't have such a cord, you can pick one up at an electronics store, though you probably want to take your camcorder with you so you can match its output jack. Your computer will need to have a video capture card. If you don't already have one, you can expect to pay about $80 to buy one, though as of this writing you can find them of various quality ranging in price from $26 to $1,000. You certainly don't need to go for the high end capture cards just for the kind of work you'll be doing with your kids.

Next you'll need a video editing program that you will use to import and digitize the video from your camcorder and then to edit the video clips together in your sequence. Video editing programs also allow you to add your voice or other sound, such as background music. Later versions of Microsoft Windows include a video editing program called Movie Maker. Many other video editing programs will allow you to download for free a trial version that should be adequate for the simple process you're working on with your kids. To buy a program, prices again range widely from as low as $40 to professional programs in the thousands. I would suggest trying a free download and if you and your kids "get hooked," buy a reasonably priced version. The editing software will come with directions and even a demonstration that will go into much more detail than is practical for me to give you here

Once you have your story, your recording of it on video, and your computer ready to digitize and edit the video, it is time to sit down and create your show. Be sure to let the kids do as much of the editing as possible. Let them learn to use the software and choose the sequence of shots. You may wind up doing a few different versions of your story as you try to refine the edits or improve the sequence. You may even find in editing that you need to shoot a couple more angles to get the smooth sequence you want. That happens to professionals all the time, though in the news business we'd usually have to compensate another way. (You can't go recreate a house fire, for instance.) Another tip: be sure to avoid what are called "jump cuts." A jump cut occurs when an object or person in one clip is suddenly in the next clip in a totally different position, one they could not possibly have moved to instantaneously. An example might be if in one clip a person has his right hand raised, but then instantly in the next clip he has his left hand raised. This is where shooting all the angles wide, medium and tight comes in handy. Editing from a wide angle of some action to a tight close-up of a hand or face can disguise the fact that the clips were not shot in immediate sequence. It can give the appearance of the smooth flow so that the viewer never has any idea they may have been shot several minutes apart.

One last thing: have fun! Enjoy the process of working together as a family!

Books:

Bias and Arrogance by Bernard Goldberg
Digital Video for Dummies by Keith Underdahl
The Educated Child by William Bennett, et al.
Hollywood Versus America by Michael Medved
Ignatius Bible (RSV)
Liberation's Children by Kay Hymowitz
Noise by Teresa Tomeo
Understanding Media by Marshall McLuhan

Online:

Decent Films - www.decentfilms.com
    (reviews by Steven D. Greydanus)
The Dove Foundation - www.dove.org
Focus on the Family - www.family.org
Howard Center for Family Religion and Society - www.profam.org
Institute for Marriage and Public Policy - www.marriagedebate.com
KidScore - http://www.mediafamily.org/kidscore/index.shtml (offers
    movie and video game reviews for parents)
Media Post - www.mediapost.com (media industry news and views;
    a great source for media research)
Media Research Center - www.mediaresearch.org
Michael Medved - www.michaelmedved.com (reviews and cultural

commentary)

National Institute on Media and the Family - www.mediafamily.org
        (media activist organization)

Parents Television Council - www.parentstv.org
        (parental television activist organization)

Screen It - www.screenit.com/index1.html
        (offers detailed movie reviews)